MY ASIAN KITCHEN

NOODLES * DUMPLINGS * SALAD * SUSHI * WOK * BAO

JENNIFER JOYCE

chartwell
books

MY ASIAN KITCHEN

NOODLES   DUMPLINGS   SALAD   SUSHI   WOK   BAO

JENNIFER JOYCE

chartwell
books

CONTENTS

WELCOME TO THE ASIAN CLASSICS, OLD AND NEW

Growing up in the United States, my childhood Asian food experiences were early limited to American-Chinese (AKA chop suey) and occasionally a travel town. I began travelling in Asia in the early 1990s that flavours of the East opened my delicious eyes of authentic Asian cooking. I this new world became acquainted with all sorts like fresh herbs, lemongrass, makrut makes, pho, potstickers, dumplings, and many. It wasn't just the hot salty-sour punch. It all too but a multitude of textures. From bitter to crunchy to pillowy soft and all was spoilt for choice at every meal. I went back to a home base. After each trip I aspired to conquer my favourite dishes, balancing flavours and textures. My, as did the result of many years of experimenting and tasting. Know we successfully cooking in my own kitchen with images you just need a solid guidance and the right ingredients.

Asian food is loved not only for their truly mouth-watering tastes, but it also has the added sense of real health benefits. Miso, soy, kombu, sesame, mushrooms and seaweed very slow and all produce is from the farm that sustain farmhouse soya beans still have a key component primarily the flavours. Asian culture is derived from the long characterized high fibre, vitamins, and beneficial nutrients such that tyramine is all about this powerful savoury filled flavour. Japanese cuisine comes from fermented beans of foods. Salt and umami are delicious and are so unique fermentation crucial primarily to the hearth of Asian cooking and they are necessary for classic Japanese curry.

In my world today, we are lucky enough to have so many ingredients widely available that once could only been decades of international travel. I dare not express the number of Asian restaurants and the development of ingredients in my educated and encouraged more adventurous home cooks. This in turn has lead to the widespread availability of products and ingredients such as yuzu juice, Sichuan peppercorns, tamarind purée and Thai chilli paste through online services and Asian superstores. To successfully replicate an authentic dish, there is usually going to be one critical flavour that is essential – whether that is togarashi, mirin or chilli bean paste. With the key items now just one click away, restaurant-quality food can be cooked up easily and enjoyably in your own kitchen.

My Asian Kitchen celebrates the classics you know and love, shows you the undiscovered and includes new modern recipes, such as healthy salads and Asian-inspired desserts. Instead of grouping recipes by country, I've arranged them by style of dish. If it's a spicy stir-fry you're after, check out the Into the Wok chapter (see page 183). If it's a comforting soup you crave, dip into Boiled & Bubbling (see page 54). Recipes are simplified, with short cuts where appropriate, but not at the expense of sacrificing flavour. I've included drawings and guides throughout the book to help you tackle difficult tasks such as folding your own dumplings, achieving the perfect grill technique or personalising your ramen and donabe hot pots.

The recipes are supplemented by a comprehensive Glossary (see page 238), which explains the uniqueness of Asian ingredients, how they differ between countries and brands and what to look for when buying.

My Asian Kitchen aims to equip you with the cooking knowledge you need to push your understanding of flavours and master your favourite dishes at home. And since Asian food is all about sharing and socialising, your friends and family are going to be pretty happy and well fed too!

Jennifer Joyce

STARTERS & SNACKS

Tempura sounds straightforward, but getting the batter right can be tricky. After many so-so results, I have finally come up with a failproof recipe. A mix of regular and fine flours, such as cornflour, blended with ice-cold soda water creates a blistering coating. The batter should never be thick – it only needs to lightly coat the vegetables or prawns, which should be sizzled to a pale colour, not browned.

PRAWN AND SWEET ONION TEMPURA

SERVES 4
PREP 10 MINUTES
COOK 10 MINUTES

3 sweet onions
250 ml (8½ fl oz) ice-cold
    soda water
1 egg
90 g (3 oz) cornflour
90 g (3 oz) plain flour, plus
    extra for dredging
vegetable oil, for frying
8 very large raw peeled prawns
    with tails, deveined

LIME PONZU SAUCE
45 ml (1½ fl oz) Japanese
    light soy sauce
2 tbsp lime juice
1 tbsp caster sugar

Peel the onions, keeping the roots intact. Slice them about 1 cm (½ inch) thick and try to keep in one piece.

Mix the lime ponzu sauce ingredients together in a small bowl and set aside.

In a large mixing bowl, mix the soda water and egg. Place the flours in another bowl. Scatter some extra plain flour onto a shallow plate and set aside.

Heat the oil in a wok or deep medium saucepan until it reaches 180–190°C (350–375°F) or when a small piece of bread instantly sizzles. I like to use a sugar thermometer to guarantee a steady temperature. If the oil is too hot, the tempura will burn and if it's too low, it will become greasy.

While the oil is heating, make the batter. Pour the dry ingredients into the wet and stir with chopsticks. Stir just enough so that it combines, but is still shaggy and lumpy. Dust the prawns and onions with the extra flour and then dip into the batter. Fry about six or seven pieces at a time and cook until golden, about 3–4 minutes. Drain on a baking tray topped with a rack. The rack maintains their crisp finish (versus paper towels, which make them soggy).

Serve the tempura immediately with the lime ponzu sauce.

NOTE
Sweet onions work best here – look for varieties such as Vidalia, Maui or Walla Walla.

I've based the flavourings in this dipping sauce on yuzo kosho, the tongue-tingling Japanese citrus paste made from pounding green chillies with salt and yuzu skin. Brushed on grilled meats or spooned into ramen or hot pots, its spicy floral taste is an epiphany. You can buy jars from Asian stores, but I've riffed a homemade version using lime zest and jalapeño, swirled here into a creamy buttermilk base.

SWEET POTATO CRISPS WITH A CREAMY CHILLI SAUCE

SERVES 4–6
PREP 10 MINUTES
COOK 45 MINUTES

2 large sweet potatoes, skin on
2 tbsp vegetable oil

CREAMY CHILLI SAUCE
1 garlic clove, sliced
½ tsp sea salt
1 thumb-sized jalapeño or other green chilli, sliced
1 tbsp yuzu or lime juice
thick zest 1 lime
60 ml (2 fl oz) mayonnaise
90 ml (3 fl oz) buttermilk

Preheat the oven to 150°C (300°F) or 130°C (250°F) fan forced. Thinly slice the well-scrubbed sweet potatoes lengthways on a mandoline, about 2.5 mm (⅒ inch) thin. They should be thicker than you might think as they will shrink and become crisp. If they are too thin, they can burn in places before they are cooked.

Rub both sides of the crisps with the oil and place on one very large baking tray or two smaller ones. Bake for 45 minutes or until crisp. You may want to swap the two trays (if using) around halfway through the cooking time. In the last 10 minutes or so of baking, flip over the potatoes so that they completely dry out.

Remove the crisps from the oven, sprinkle with sea salt and leave to cool on the tray. If not eating immediately, place in a tin or sealed container and line the base with baking paper so it absorbs any moisture to keep them crisp.

To make the creamy chilli sauce, in a mortar and pestle, crush the garlic, salt, green chilli, yuzu or lime juice and lime zest until they form a paste. Scrape into a small serving bowl and add the mayonnaise and buttermilk. Stir to combine.

Serve the creamy chilli sauce with the potato crisps.

NOTE
This is also a perfect dip for the Miso kale crisps on page 14, some steamed edamame or fresh crudités.

You may want to make a double batch of these addictive chips as they disappear quickly. Try to use big leaves of kale, with the stems removed, and then rip or cut into pieces. The pre-cut bags include the tough, woody stems, so avoid those as the stems don't go crisp like the leaves. Wasabi can be used in place of the miso, but reduce the quantity by half.

MISO KALE CRISPS

SERVES 4–6
PREP 10 MINUTES
COOK 20 MINUTES

1 tbsp pale (shiro) miso
2 tbsp rice vinegar
2 tbsp melted coconut oil
150 g (5½ oz) kale or cavolo nero
1 tbsp togarashi or furikake
   spice mix

Preheat the oven to 150°C (300°F) or 130°C (250°F) fan forced. In a large bowl, mix the miso, rice vinegar and coconut oil together.

Remove the stems from the kale or cavolo nero and cut the leaves into 6 cm (2½ inch) pieces. Add the kale leaves to the miso mixture and massage it into the leaves.

Place the kale in a single layer on a large baking tray or two smaller ones. Sprinkle with the spice mix and bake for 20 minutes or until crisp.

NOTE
The Miso kale crisps are pictured on page 13 alongside the Sweet potato crisps.

For very little work this creates a momentous starter. Dice up some spanking-fresh scallops with mango and toss with a Thai-inspired coconut dressing – your mouth will light up like a pinball machine. Serve with Thai rice crackers to scoop up with or you could make a batch of the lotus wafers on page 44.

COCONUT MANGO SCALLOP TARTARE *WITH* RICE CRACKERS

SERVES 4
PREP 20 MINUTES, PLUS
1 HOUR CHILLING

300 g (10½ oz) scallops
150 ml (5 fl oz) lime juice
2 tbsp orange juice
2 tbsp finely diced red onion
½ tsp sea salt
1 tsp caster sugar
1 ripe but firm mango
2 small Thai chillies or 1 thumb-sized
   red chilli, thinly sliced
small handful chopped
   coriander (cilantro)

COCONUT DRESSING
50 ml (2 fl oz) coconut cream
zest and juice 1 lime
1 tbsp fish sauce
1 tsp grated ginger

Thai rice crackers, to serve

Cut the scallops into 1 cm (½ inch) pieces and place in a bowl with the lime and orange juices, red onion, sea salt and sugar. Combine well, then cover and refrigerate for 1 hour.

Drain the scallops, then toss gently in a bowl with all the coconut dressing ingredients.

Cut the mango into 1 cm (½ inch) pieces, add to the bowl with the chilli and coriander and toss to combine well. Serve with the Thai rice crackers.

NOTE
Halibut or another firm, mild white fish can also be used.

A few years ago just outside the Tsukiji fish market in Tokyo, I discovered tamagoyaki. An omelette made from rolled up layers of sweet egg, it's a snack, sushi component or part of a bento box. Mesmerised by a street stall with eight pans on the go, I was inspired to try it at home. They served it up with a nostril-flaring hot mustard, but I've concocted a more mellow version using a little miso.

JAPANESE OMELETTE SQUARES ‹TAMAGOYAKI› WITH SWEET MUSTARD

SERVES 4
PREP 5 MINUTES
COOK 10 MINUTES

4 eggs, beaten
1 tbsp mirin
2 tsp caster sugar
½ tsp Japanese
   light soy sauce
1 tsp vegetable oil
1 tbsp finely chopped chives,
   for sprinkling

SWEET MUSTARD SAUCE
1 tbsp hot yellow mustard
2 tbsp mirin
1 tsp pale (shiro) miso
1 tbsp rice vinegar
2 tsp honey

Mix the sweet mustard sauce ingredients together in a small bowl and set aside.

In a medium bowl, add all the remaining ingredients, except the oil and chives, together with a pinch of salt. Whisk until smooth. Pour into two small bowls so you can make two pancakes.

Heat a medium frying pan or, even better, a rectangular tamagoyaki frying pan. Brush the oil over the bottom of the pan. Keep the pan over a low–medium heat and pour in a thin layer of the egg mixture from one of the bowls.

Using two spatulas, roll the egg up after 30 seconds while it's still slightly gooey. Push it to the end of the pan and pour in another thin layer of egg. While it's still slightly wet, roll up the omelette over the new egg. Repeat the process until you have used up all the egg, then slide onto a plate. Repeat with the second omelette.

Let the omelettes cool for a minute and then cut into 2.5 cm (1 inch) squares. Sprinkle with the chives and serve with the sweet mustard dipping sauce.

NOTE
A normal non-stick frying pan works fine here, but you can buy the little rectangular omelette frying pans at Muji for not much money.

Eaten for breakfast or as a snack all over China, spring onion pancakes are made from the same dough as dumplings. They're rolled out in a method similar to a roti – the dough is brushed with sesame oil, showered in spring onions, rolled up and twisted like a snake, and then rolled again. Pan-fry them until golden to create their chewy yet flaky texture and then dip into a tangy red chilli sauce to eat.

CHINESE SPRING ONION PANCAKES

SERVES 4
PREP 20 MINUTES, PLUS
30 MINUTES RESTING
COOK 10 MINUTES

350 g (12 oz) plain flour
225 ml (8 fl oz) boiling water
3 tbsp sesame oil
8 spring onions (scallions),
    chopped
1 thumb-sized red chilli, sliced
1 tbsp sesame seeds, toasted

sriracha or Chinese red chilli
    sauce, to serve

Tip the flour into a food processor or large mixing bowl. With the motor running or using a spoon to stir, pour in the boiling water. The dough will come together into a ball. Remove it from the machine or bowl. Knead on a clean work surface for about 5 minutes until the dough is smooth. Place in a bowl, cover with plastic wrap and let rest for 30 minutes.

Slice the dough into four pieces and roll each one out on a lightly floured surface into a 20 cm (8 inch) circle. Brush the surface of each with some of the sesame oil. Sprinkle with all of the spring onions and red chilli.

Roll each circle up into a tight log. Twist each log around itself like a snake to make a circle. Roll each circle out again to about 18 cm (7 inches). Keep the finished pancakes separated with baking paper and covered with a tea towel.

Heat a large frying pan and add some of the remaining sesame oil. Fry one of the pancakes for about 2 minutes until golden on one side, and then flip over. Repeat with the remaining three, adding oil to the pan each time. Cut the pancakes into squares or triangles.

Sprinkle the pancakes with the sesame seeds and serve with sriracha or Chinese red chilli sauce.

NOTE
My favourite sriracha sauce is Sriraja Panich, a Thai brand. If your sauce is too hot, then add a teaspoon or so of rice vinegar to soften the heat.

I've spent many years trying to perfect my method for the ultimate fried squid. Two factors make all the difference: scoring the flesh with a sharp knife, and using a mixture of rice flour and cornflour to dust before frying. The finer flour produces an ultra-crisp finish.

SALT-AND-PEPPER CRISPY SQUID with SWEET-AND-HOT CHILLI JAM

SERVES 4
PREP 15 MINUTES
COOK 10 MINUTES

400 g (14 oz) baby squid
vegetable oil, for frying
2 thumb-sized red chillies, sliced
3 spring onions (scallions), chopped

SWEET-AND-HOT CHILLI JAM
4 thumb-sized red chillies, chopped
3 garlic cloves
1 tsp chopped ginger
150 ml (5 fl oz) rice vinegar
100 g (3½ oz) caster sugar
2 tbsp lime juice

SALT-AND-PEPPER FLOUR
2 tbsp Sichuan peppercorns
2 tsp black peppercorns
1 tbsp sea salt
1 tbsp red chilli flakes
75 g (2½ oz) mixed rice flour
   and cornflour

To make the chilli jam, in a food processor pulse the chillies, garlic and ginger until finely chopped. Scrape into a small saucepan and add the vinegar, sugar and 60 ml (2 fl oz) water. Bring to a boil and cook until it forms a thin syrup. Remove from the heat and add the lime juice.

To make the salt-and-pepper flour, in a small dry frying pan toast all the peppercorns for about 30 seconds or until fragrant. Crush with a mortar and pestle or a spice grinder and then mix in a shallow dish with the sea salt, chilli flakes and flours.

Separate the cleaned and dried squid tentacles from the bodies. Slice the bodies and lay out flat, then score the flesh with a criss-cross pattern. Cut into 4 cm (1½ inch) pieces. Dust the squid bodies and tentacles with the salt-and-pepper flour.

Heat the oil in a wok or deep medium saucepan until it reaches 180–190°C (350–375°F) or when a small piece of bread instantly sizzles. Fry eight to ten pieces of squid at a time until golden, about 2 minutes. Drain on paper towels.

Add the chilli slices to the wok and fry for 30 seconds until crisp (you could also fry up some sliced garlic, which never hurts).

Serve the hot crispy squid with spring onions and fried chillies sprinkled over and the chilli jam on the side.

VIETNAMESE RICE PAPER ROLLS

USE

MINT, BASIL AND
CORIANDER (CILANTRO)

FRUIT

VEGGIES

PRAWNS, PORK, BEEF
OR CHICKEN

RICE VERMICELLI

1

Place a wrapper into warm water and leave for 30 seconds. Pull out when wrinkly but still firm.
Too long = too sticky. Start over!

2

Place the filling on lower half of the wrapper – it should be about 7.5 cm (3 inches) wide and 2.5 cm (1 inch) high.

3

Bring the lower half up and over the filling.
Roll over once, keeping the tension tight.

4

Bring the sides in, leaving no holes.

5

Roll up and keep the tension tight.

=

READY FOR DIPPING SAUCE!

SWEET CHILLI
NUOC CHAM
LIME CHILLI
PEANUT SAUCE
= RECOMMENDED!

You can have a lot of fun with these colourful, ultra-healthy spring rolls. Any vegetables can be used, so let the left side of your brain take control. After a few tries you will get the hang of rolling, but I have a few tips to make it easier: err on the side of not soaking the wrappers for too long, don't overfill the rolls and keep the tension up when rolling so they are tight.

RAINBOW VIETNAMESE RICE PAPER ROLLS

MAKES 8 ROLLS
PREP 1 HOUR

100 g (3½ oz) thin rice vermicelli
2 baby cucumbers
100 g (3½ oz) cooked peeled
    prawns, halved lengthways
1 mango, sliced
1 papaya, sliced
3 heritage carrots, julienned
2 shallots, thinly sliced
handful each mint, coriander
    (cilantro) and basil leaves
12 round rice paper wrappers
    (15 cm/6 inches)

LIME CHILLI DIPPING SAUCE
2 tbsp fish sauce
4 tbsp lime juice
2 tsp grated ginger
2 tbsp orange juice
1 red chilli, sliced
1 garlic clove, finely chopped

Soak the rice vermicelli in warm water until softened, then drain.

Mix the lime chilli dipping sauce ingredients together and pour into a serving bowl.

Slice the baby cucumbers into ribbons using a potato peeler. Place the cucumber, prawns, mango, papaya, carrot, shallot, herbs and vermicelli in separate piles on a tray. That way when you start rolling, you will have everything ready to go.

Place a large tea towel on a work surface. Pour warm water into a bowl. Drop one rice paper wrapper at a time into the water for about 30 seconds. When soft but still a little stiff, remove the wrappers and place on the tea towel (don't pat dry on top as this will make them too sticky).

Place a line of two prawns, mango or papaya, carrot, shallot, noodles, mint, coriander and basil on the lower half of the wrapper. Bring the lower part of the wrapper up and over the filling, then fold the sides in, leaving no holes, and roll up tightly.

To make cucumber rolls, place three cucumber slices vertically across the middle of each wrapper. Place your filling in the same place as above and then roll up.

Place the rice paper rolls seam side down on a tray lined with baking paper. Throw away any wrapper that rips and start again with a fresh one. It may take a few to get the knack, so don't get discouraged. If the wrapper is too soft, it will fall apart, and if it's too hard, it will not stick together. Practise a few so you can get a feel for the right consistency.

To serve, cut the spring rolls in half and serve with the lime chilli dipping sauce.

NOTE

You can store the rolls for up to 12 hours before serving. Cover the finished rolls with baking paper and then wrap the entire tray in plastic wrap. Keep refrigerated until ready to use.

This creation was inspired by Japan's smoke-filled izakaya – a kind of pub where uber snacks like charcoal-grilled yakitori and fried karaage chicken rule. Shichimi togarashi, a citrus, chilli and sesame seed spice, gives these sticky soy wings a fruity kick with a mild heat. Find it in Asian stores, online or make your own (see Glossary page 238). Serve the wings with lots of napkins and ice-cold beers.

SOY, LEMON *and* TOGARASHI CHICKEN WINGS

SERVES 4
PREP 10 MINUTES, PLUS 2 HOURS MARINATING
COOK 45 MINUTES

60 ml (2 fl oz) Japanese light soy sauce
60 ml (2 fl oz) sake or mirin
60 ml (2 fl oz) honey
1 tbsp grated ginger
2 garlic cloves, crushed
juice 1 lemon
2 tbsp togarashi spice mix
1.4 kg (3 lb) chicken wings, halved

Preheat the oven to 200°C (400°F) or 180°C (350°F) fan forced.

In a small bowl, mix the soy, sake or mirin, honey, ginger, garlic, lemon juice and togarashi together, reserving 1 tablespoon each of the soy sauce, honey and togarashi.

Place the wings in a zip lock bag or bowl with the marinade and marinate for 2 hours or refrigerate overnight.

Place the chicken on a large baking tray with the marinade. Cover with foil and bake for 15 minutes. Remove the foil and bake for another 30 minutes.

In the last 10 minutes of the cooking time, drizzle the reserved honey and soy over the wings. The wings are ready when they are sticky and crisp at the edges. Sprinkle with the remaining spice mixture. Serve hot with lots of napkins.

NOTE

You can buy chicken wings already cut in half, ask your butcher to prepare them or it's easy to do it yourself. Pick up a wing and snap back the joint as if you were bending it backwards. Use a pair of poultry or other clean scissors to cut through the knuckle and separate each wing into two pieces.

Even though the name suggests the origins of this dish lie in old colonial Burma, this is 100 percent an American invention. Firmly planted onto most Chinese menus in the States, these have become classic dumplings – and rightly so because they are damn good. Cream cheese, crab meat and plump spring onions are wrapped in wonton dough and deep fried until golden and crisp.

CRAB RANGOONS

MAKES 20 DUMPLINGS
PREP 30 MINUTES
COOK 5 MINUTES

100 g (3½ oz) fresh white crab meat
125 g (4 oz) cream cheese
2 spring onions (scallions),
    thinly sliced
1 small red chilli, diced
40 square wonton wrappers
1 egg white
vegetable oil, for frying

sriracha or other hot chilli sauce,
    to serve

Mix the crab, cream cheese, spring onion, chilli and some sea salt and freshly ground black pepper in a small mixing bowl.

Place 20 wonton wrappers on a clean tea towel with a corner facing towards you. Brush the wrappers with egg white. Place a second wonton on top of each brushed wrapper, creating a double thickness.

Place a teaspoon of filling in the middle of each wrapper. Brush egg white around all sides of the wrapper. Bring the two opposite corners together to the middle and pinch together. Then bring up the other two corners towards the middle as well so that it looks like a roof. Pinch all four edges so they are sealed. Repeat with all the wrappers until you have 20 wontons.

Heat the oil in a wok or deep medium saucepan until it reaches 180–190°C (350–375°F) or when a small piece of bread instantly sizzles. Fry five wontons at a time until they are crisp. Drain on paper towels.

Serve immediately with hot chilli sauce.

Tofu comes into its own with this crisp salt-and-pepper coating, which seals in the marshmallow-soft interior. Stock up on good firm tofu, packed in water, as it keeps for ages in the fridge. Asian stores sell the best quality or buy it online. If you aren't a soya bean lover, then you can slot in prawns or chicken pieces with the same delicious preparation.

SICHUAN PEPPER TOFU *WITH* BLACK VINEGAR DIPPING SAUCE

SERVES 4
PREP 15 MINUTES
COOK 15 MINUTES

400 g (14 oz) firm tofu, drained
1 tbsp Sichuan peppercorns
50 g (2 oz) cornflour
1 tbsp red chilli flakes
1 tbsp sea salt
250 ml (8½ fl oz) vegetable oil
2 thumb-sized red chillies, sliced
2 garlic cloves, thinly sliced
2 spring onions (scallions), chopped

BLACK VINEGAR DIPPING SAUCE
2 tbsp roasted chilli flakes
   in oil, drained
1 tbsp black vinegar
1 tbsp light soy sauce
1 tbsp hoisin sauce

RED CHILLI DIPPING SAUCE
3 tbsp sriracha or
   other hot chilli sauce
1 tbsp rice vinegar

Wrap a thick layer of paper towels around the tofu. Weigh down with a plate and then as soon as the towels are wet, replace with more. Repeat about three times until the tofu has shrunk a bit and is well drained. This is a very important step as the drier the tofu is, the crisper it will fry up. Slice into 4 cm (1½ inch) cubes.

In a small frying pan, heat the Sichuan peppercorns for about 30 seconds until fragrant. Roughly grind in a spice mill or with a mortar and pestle and then mix in a small bowl with the cornflour, chilli flakes, sea salt and a good grinding of black pepper. Toss the tofu in the flour and coat well. Shake off any excess.

In two small bowls, mix the black vinegar and red chilli dipping sauce ingredients.

When you are close to eating, heat a large wok or big frying pan. Add the oil and fry the tofu in batches until crisp on all sides. Drain on paper towels.

Add the chilli and garlic to the hot oil and fry for 1 minute or until golden and crisp.

Serve the hot tofu with the dipping sauces and a sprinkle of the chilli, garlic and spring onions.

FRiED
SPRiNG ROLLS

1

Point one corner of a wrapper towards you and brush the surface with egg white. Place a second wrapper on top and brush again.

2

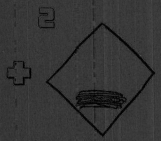

Add the filling to the lower third of the wrapper, leaving plenty of space around it.

3

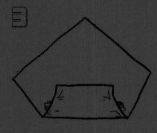

Bring the lower corner up and roll over once. Keep the tension tight!

4

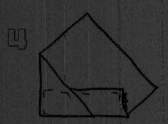

Fold the left corner over and press.

5

Bring the other corner over to create an envelope shape.

6

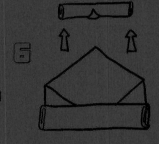

Roll up all the way, still keeping the tension tight.

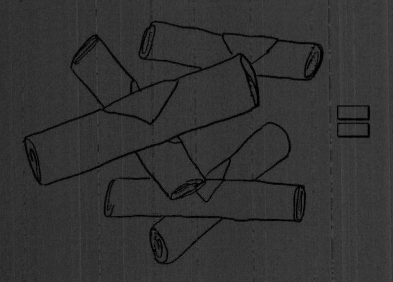

=

READY FOR DEEP FRYING!

Where I grew up in Wisconsin there weren't many Asian restaurants, but we did have a few Chinese joints. Most served bland chop suey and other typical takeaway dishes, but there was one gem that stuck in my mind – fat spring rolls served with little packets of spicy mustard sauce. I didn't encounter this combination on my China travels, but this American riff gets my vote.

CHINESE SPRING ROLLS
WITH SWEET MUSTARD

MAKES 10–12 SPRING ROLLS
PREP 45 MINUTES
COOK 10 MINUTES

1 tbsp vegetable oil
2 garlic cloves, finely chopped
3 cm (1¼ inch) ginger, chopped
150 g (5 oz) cabbage, shredded
2 large carrots, julienned
100 g (3½ oz) bean sprouts
100 g (3½ oz) shiitake
   mushrooms, sliced
1 celery stalk, julienned
4 spring onions (scallions), chopped
1 tbsp light soy sauce
2 tsp cornflour
24 spring roll wrappers
   (15 cm/6 inches)
2 egg whites
peanut (groundnut) oil, for frying
Sweet mustard sauce (see page 16)

Heat the vegetable oil in a wok or sauté pan. Add the garlic, ginger, cabbage, carrot, bean sprouts, shiitake mushrooms, celery and spring onions. Sauté for 3–4 minutes until softened and then add the soy sauce mixed with the cornflour. Remove from the heat and scrape into a bowl. Refrigerate until completely cool. Drain off any excess liquid.

On a clean surface, place two spring roll wrappers on top of one another (this helps make the shell extra crisp as the filling is slightly wet). It is easiest to position the wrappers with one corner facing towards you. Brush some of the egg white across the whole surface. Place about 3 tablespoons of the filling on the lower third of the wrapper. Bring the lower tip up and fold over the filling. Fold in the side flaps and roll tightly into a spring roll. It's VERY important to keep the tension as you roll so it's tight. Brush the finshed roll with egg white along the seal. The rolls can be refrigerated for up to 4 hours, layered between non-stick baking paper, and then wrapped in plastic wrap, or immediately frozen.

Heat the oil in a wok or deep medium saucepan until it reaches 180–190°C (350–375°F) or when a small piece of bread instantly sizzles. Fry five or six spring rolls at a time until crispy and drain on paper towels. Keep the cooked rolls in a warm oven.

Serve the spring rolls immediately with the mustard sauce.

NOTE
If you have frozen the spring rolls raw, then you can cook straight from the freezer. They spit oil a bit, but will end up just as crisp.

Pale imitations of Cantonese prawn toast abound, but when made properly it's one of the greatest Chinese snacks. This preparation is golden for two reasons: slivers of water chestnuts impart a sweet crunch and sourdough bread ensures there is no soggy base.

PRAWN TOASTS *with* WATER CHESTNUTS *and* SPRING ONIONS

MAKES 30 TOASTS
PREP 10 MINUTES
COOK 10 MINUTES

300 g (10½ oz) raw
    peeled prawns
75 g (2½ oz) drained
    water chestnuts
1 tsp chopped ginger
1 tsp light soy sauce
1 egg white
1 tsp cornflour
4 spring onions (scallions), chopped
10 slices white sourdough
50 g (2 oz) black and white
    sesame seeds
vegetable oil, for frying

sriracha or other hot chilli sauce
    and/or Black vinegar dipping
    sauce (see page 29), to serve

Place the prawns, water chestnuts, ginger, soy, egg white, cornflour and 2 spring onions in a food processor and pulse until chunky. Remove and set aside.

Remove the crusts from the bread and cut each slice into three triangles. Spread the mixture thickly over the bread slices. Dip each one in the sesame seeds.

Fill a wok or small, deep heavy pan with 5 cm (2 inches) of oil. Line a baking tray with a layer of paper towels for draining.

Heat the oil in a wok or deep medium saucepan until it reaches 180–190°C (350–375°F) or when a small piece of bread instantly sizzles. Fry five or six toasts at a time until golden and crisp, about 1–2 minutes.

Serve the prawn toasts with the sriracha sauce and/or black vinegar dipping sauce.

Before I visited Japan I never thought much of agedashi – it was either too oily or the stock was bland. But after enjoying the real deal, I finally understood what the fuss was about. Making dashi stock is SO worth the effort and will transform this dish. Silken tofu is traditional, but it's very tricky to coat in cornflour without breaking up. Medium-firm tofu works better and still produces a creamy result.

AGEDASHI TOFU

SERVES 4
PREP 15 MINUTES, PLUS
20 MINUTES PRESSING
COOK 15 MINUTES

400 g (14 oz) medium-firm
  tofu, drained
45 ml (1½ fl oz) Japanese
  light soy sauce
45 ml (1½ fl oz) mirin
300 ml (10 fl oz) Dashi stock
  (see page 78)
vegetable oil, for frying
50 g (2 oz) cornflour
2 spring onions (scallions),
  finely chopped
1 thumb-sized red chilli,
  finely sliced
3 tsp grated ginger
1 sheet nori, shredded

Wrap the tofu in a clean tea towel. Place a tray on top and weigh down with something heavy like tins or a pan. Leave for 20 minutes to press, changing the tea towel if necessary to remove as much water as possible.

In a saucepan, simmer the soy sauce, mirin and dashi together. Keep the sauce warm.

Heat the oil in a wok or deep medium saucepan until it reaches 180–190°C (350–375°F) or when a small piece of bread instantly sizzles. Slice the tofu into 12 squares and coat with the cornflour. Deep fry half the cubes for a few minutes until pale golden, then remove and drain on a rack or paper towels. Repeat with the remaining cubes.

Place three pieces of tofu in each of four small bowls and pour the sauce over. Top with spring onion, chilli and grated ginger. Sprinkle with the nori and serve immediately.

The genius of Vietnamese food is how it packs in so much taste while still retaining feather-light freshness. Blitz these prawn cakes in the food processor, grill with a brushing of palm sugar glaze and eat wrapped up in cold, crisp lettuce leaves with a sticky peanut chilli sauce for dipping.

PRAWN CAKES *WITH* PEANUT CHILLI SAUCE

MAKES 16 SMALL CAKES
PREP 15 MINUTES
COOK 10 MINUTES

2 tbsp palm or soft brown sugar
3 cm (1¼ inch) ginger
handful coriander
  (cilantro), chopped
3 small Thai shallots, thinly sliced
1 thumb-sized red chilli, diced
400 g (14 oz) raw peeled prawns
zest 2 limes
1 tbsp fish sauce
3 tsp vegetable oil

PEANUT CHILLI SAUCE
100 g (3½ oz) caster sugar
100 ml (3½ fl oz) rice vinegar
2 red chillies, diced
2 tbsp peanuts, toasted,
  finely chopped
2 small Thai shallots, chopped
1 tbsp fish sauce
1 tbsp chopped coriander (cilantro)

chilled iceberg lettuce, to serve

In a small frying pan, mix the palm or brown sugar with 1 tablespoon water. Bring to a boil and then remove from the heat.

To make the peanut chilli sauce, boil the sugar and vinegar in a small saucepan with a pinch of salt. Bring to a boil and simmer for about 5 minutes until syrupy. Remove from the heat and let cool completely. Add the chilli, peanuts, shallot, fish sauce and coriander.

To make the prawn cakes, place the ginger, coriander, shallot and chilli in a food processor and blend until fine. Add the prawns, lime zest and fish sauce and pulse until combined, being sure not to blend too fine as the texture should be nice and chunky. Grind plenty of black pepper over it.

Using oiled hands, form the prawn mixture into 16 flat cakes. Refrigerate until ready to cook.

Preheat the grill. Brush both sides of the prawn cakes with a tiny bit of oil and put on a rack placed on top of a baking tray.

Grill the cakes for 1 minute, then brush the tops with the palm sugar syrup. Cook for another 2–3 minutes or until opaque. You won't need to turn them as they cook fast. Serve the warm cakes with the chilled lettuce leaves and peanut chilli sauce.

TEMAKI HAND ROLLS

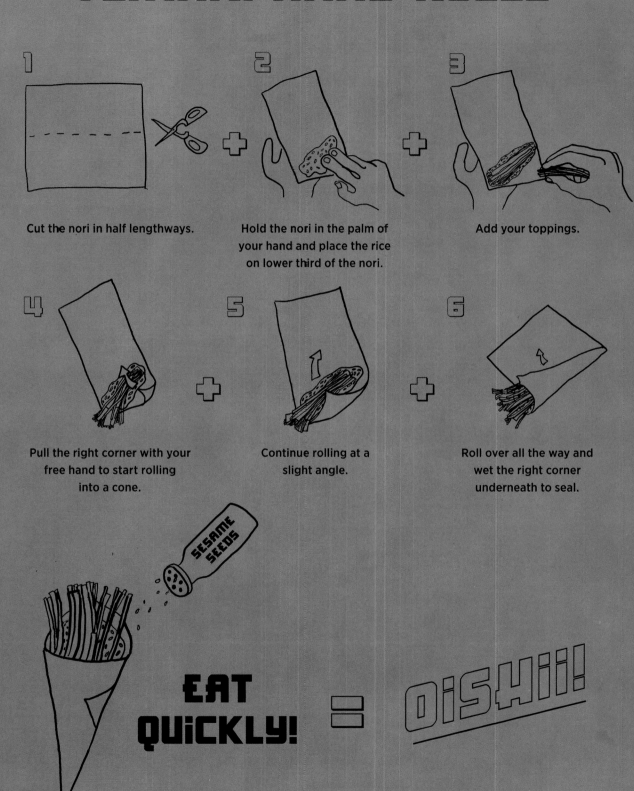

1 Cut the nori in half lengthways.

2 Hold the nori in the palm of your hand and place the rice on lower third of the nori.

3 Add your toppings.

4 Pull the right corner with your free hand to start rolling into a cone.

5 Continue rolling at a slight angle.

6 Roll over all the way and wet the right corner underneath to seal.

SESAME SEEDS

EAT QUICKLY! = OiSHii!

Temaki are nori-wrapped sushi ice cream cones filled with crab, prawns, chicken or whatever deliciousness your heart desires. I like to pop in some spicy mayo and vegetables alongside the sushi rice to give colour and flavour. If you enjoy making these I would strongly suggest buying a small rice maker as it cooks the rice perfectly. It's one appliance I use everyday – it won't gather dust in a cupboard.

JAPANESE HAND ROLL SUSHI ‹TEMAKI›

MAKES 8 ROLLS
PREP 15 MINUTES

250 g (9 oz) Japanese rice
4 sheets nori
200 g (7 oz) tuna fillet
3 tsp togarashi or furikake spice mix
2 tbsp rice vinegar
2 tsp caster sugar
8 large pieces pickled ginger
small bunch chives
1 carrot or cucumber, julienned
1 avocado, sliced into 8
sesame seeds, to garnish (optional)

SPICY MAYO
2 tbsp Kewpie or
    regular mayonnaise
1 tsp yuzu or lime juice
1 tbsp hot chilli sauce

Cook the rice according to the manufacturer's instructions.

Use a pair of scissors to cut the nori in half lengthways so you have eight rectangles.

Slice the fish into 16 pieces, about 1 x 8 cm (½ x 3 inches). Sprinkle with the togarashi so they are covered on all sides.

In a small bowl, mix the rice vinegar and sugar with a pinch of salt. When the sugar has dissolved, pour this over your warm rice and gently mix until it is absorbed and cooled.

To make the spicy mayo, in a small bowl mix the mayonnaise with the yuzu or lime and the chilli sauce. Lay out all the remaining ingredients so you can begin rolling.

Place a heaped tablespoon of the rice on the lower third of one of the nori rectangles. Arrange the rice so it's at an angle and you can still pick up the corner of the nori paper. Spread a few teaspoons of spicy mayo over the rice, then arrange the pickled ginger, a few chives, two pieces of the fish, the carrot and the avocado next to it. Sprinkle over a few sesame seeds (optional).

Roll the cone up, starting on the right side so that it rolls slightly at an angle. Wet the right corner underneath to seal. Arrange on a serving board or plate and eat soon after making.

NOTE
Be sure to buy tuna fillet with little or no marbling. You could also use salmon.

If there were ever two ingredients that were meant for each other, it would be tuna and avocado. Their sweet, mild taste and vibrant colours are perfect for sashimi, drizzled here with a sharp orange and yuzu dressing. The homemade crisp lotus wafers break up the soft texture, but feel free to substitute bought ones or rice crackers, both of which can be found at Asian stores.

TUNA SASHIMI *with* AVOCADO *and* CITRUS DRESSING

SERVES 4
PREP 15 MINUTES
COOK 15 MINUTES

300 g (10½ oz) ruby red tuna loin
3 tbsp black sesame seeds
1 large ripe avocado
4 radishes, sliced
2 tbsp finely chopped chives

LOTUS WAFERS
2 lotus roots, peeled
2 tbsp vegetable oil

CITRUS DRESSING
3 tsp Japanese light soy sauce
2 tbsp lime juice
2 tbsp orange juice
1 small shallot, finely diced
2 tbsp yuzu juice
2 tsp caster sugar
2 tsp finely grated ginger

Preheat the oven to 200°C (400°F) or 180°C (350°F) fan forced.

Using a mandoline, slice the lotus root for the wafers about 3 mm (⅛ inch) thick. They should be thicker than you might expect as they will shrink and become crisp. If they are too thin, they will burn. Arrange in a single layer over a clean tea towel or paper towels. Cover with another towel and press to remove the water.

Place the lotus slices on a baking tray and brush with oil on both sides. Bake for 15 minutes until crisp and golden. Remove from the tray and sprinkle with sea salt.

Slice the tuna into 10 cm (4 inch) long steaks. Roll each cylinder of tuna in the sesame seeds and then thinly slice.

Halve the avocado and remove the pit. Cut thin slices of the flesh, cutting right down to the skin. Use a large soup spoon to remove the slices. Alternatively you can use an egg slicer, but you will need to remove the skin first.

To make the citrus dressing, combine all the ingredients in a small bowl. Some soy sauce is saltier than others, so taste to see if you need to add more citrus juice or sugar.

On a long platter or individual plates, arrange the tuna slices and the avocado. Top with the radishes and pour the dressing over. Sprinkle with the chives and serve with the lotus wafers.

NOTE

If you are making the sashimi ahead of serving, place the tuna slices on a plate lined with baking paper and loosely cover with more baking paper. Don't use plastic wrap as it makes the fish sweat.

Taiwanese night markets are filled with stalls and street hawkers selling their famous 'popcorn' chicken. Not just your average fried snack, the five-spice marinade and chilli salt sprinkle separate this fried chicken from the rest of the pack.

TAIWANESE FRIED CHICKEN

SERVES 4
**PREP 15 MINUTES, PLUS
1 HOUR MARINATING**
COOK 10 MINUTES

1 tbsp light soy sauce
1 tbsp Shaoxing rice wine
2 garlic cloves, crushed
3 tsp grated ginger
2 tsp five-spice powder
500 g (1 lb 2 oz) boneless
   skinless chicken thighs
1 tsp Sichuan peppercorns
1 tsp red chilli flakes
½ tsp sea salt
100 g (3½ oz) rice flour
   or cornflour
vegetable oil, for frying
1 large handful Thai or regular basil

SPICY DIPPING SAUCE
1 tbsp light soy sauce
1 tbsp black or rice vinegar
2 tsp sambal oelek, sriracha or
   other chilli sauce

In a shallow glass dish or zip lock bag, mix the soy, rice wine, garlic, ginger and five-spice powder. Cut any excess fat off the chicken and slice into bite-size pieces. Place in the dish or bag with the marinade and mix together. Leave for at least 1 hour or overnight, refrigerated.

Drain the chicken and discard the marinade.

Toast the Sichuan peppercorns in a small frying pan and then crush with a mortar and pestle or in a spice grinder. Mix with the chilli flakes and sea salt and set aside.

Mix all the spicy dipping sauce ingredients together in a small bowl and set aside.

Place the rice flour or cornflour in a shallow dish and dip the chicken into the flour, coating well. Shake off the excess and place the chicken on a clean plate.

Heat the oil in a wok or deep medium saucepan until it reaches 180–190°C (350–375°F) or when a small piece of bread instantly sizzles. You don't want the oil too hot or the chicken will turn brown too quickly. Fry the chicken in batches, about eight or nine pieces at a time, until golden. Drain on paper towels. Throw the basil leaves into the oil for 30 seconds until crisp, then drain.

Place the chicken on a serving dish and scatter with the basil and a sprinkle of the Sichuan chilli salt. Serve with the spicy dipping sauce on the side.

Tataki is one step away from raw, but involves a quick searing before thinly slicing. To avoid the fragile pieces falling apart, I wrap the beef tightly in plastic wrap after browning and refrigerate before slicing. The garlic chips take this Japanese classic up a level, but if you don't have time, the ponzu onion dressing still makes this dish.

BEEF TATAKI *with* GARLIC CHIPS *and* PONZU ONION DRESSING

SERVES 4
PREP 20 MINUTES, PLUS
2 HOURS CHILLING
COOK 5 MINUTES

300 g (10½ oz) beef fillet
1 tbsp vegetable oil
1 tbsp chopped chives

PONZU ONION DRESSING
4 tsp Japanese light soy sauce
2 tbsp finely diced shallots
45 ml (1½ fl oz) yuzu juice
1 tbsp caster sugar
2 tsp grated ginger

GARLIC CHIPS
3 garlic cloves
125 ml (4½ fl oz) vegetable oil

Slice the meat into two 10 cm (4 inch) long cylindrical pieces. Season the beef well using lots of sea salt and freshly ground pepper. Heat a frying pan with the vegetable oil and sear the meat on all sides until it is browned and sealed, about 2–3 minutes. Remove from the pan and let cool for a few minutes. Wrap the beef very tightly in plastic wrap and refrigerate for at least 2 hours and up to 24 hours ahead.

Mix the ponzu onion dressing ingredients together in a small bowl and set aside.

To make the garlic chips, finely slice the garlic on a mandoline or using a sharp knife. Add the oil and garlic to a small frying pan or small saucepan. Keep the heat on medium–low and let the garlic slowly get crisp. Remove with a slotted spoon when golden and let dry on paper towels. Sprinkle with salt. You can make these chips a day in advance and keep in a covered container lined with a small piece of baking paper.

Thinly slice the beef, arrange on a platter and pour the dressing over. Top with the garlic chips and chives and serve.

NOTES

Be sure to avoid any garlic cloves that have a green kernel inside as it is very bitter.

It sounds strange not to heat the oil first when frying the garlic, but it's a very successful method for getting the garlic crisp and evenly cooked.

PiCKLES

YELLOW PiCKLED RADiSH

SERVES 4
PREP 10 MINUTES
COOK 5 MINUTES

Pickles harmonise and complement almost any Asian dish. Their sourness offsets the salty soy and rich flavours and they are the finishing touch for any soup or fried food or as a side alongside barbecued meat. These crisp radish pickles are a beautiful yellow and have a mild brine of rice vinegar.

250 g (9 oz) mooli (white radish), peeled
1 tbsp salt
100 ml (3½ fl oz) rice vinegar
½ tsp ground turmeric
50 g (2 oz) caster sugar

Cut the mooli into 5 mm (¼ inch) slices.

In a medium saucepan, bring 100 ml (3½ fl oz) water, the salt, rice vinegar, turmeric and sugar to a boil. Add the radish and turn off the heat. Let cool to room temperature and then place in a sterilised jar or covered container.

NOTE
For a pink variation, chop the mooli into batons and add 3 slices of raw or cooked beetroot to the container. Don't add the turmeric to the brine.

JAPANESE CARROT PiCKLES

SERVES 4
PREP 10 MINUTES
COOK 5 MINUTES

You can use any hard vegetable for this recipe: try green beans, beetroot or blanched cauliflower. The vegetables don't require pre-salting, so you can just add them raw to the boiled brine.

300 g (10½ oz) carrots (about 3)
250 ml (8½ fl oz) rice vinegar
2 slices ginger
1 tsp coriander seeds
1 tsp red chilli flakes
1 tbsp sea salt
50 g (2 oz) caster sugar

Cut the carrots into 1.5 cm (⅝ inch) batons.

In a medium saucepan, heat the rice vinegar, ginger, coriander seeds, chilli flakes, salt and sugar. Bring to a boil and then add the carrots. Leave to cool completely and then refrigerate in a sterilised jar or covered container.

QUICK KOREAN CUCUMBER PICKLES

SERVES 4
PREP 10 MINUTES

If you aren't up for making homemade kimchee, toss together a bowl of these (see photo on page 140).

3 baby cucumbers
1 tbsp white sesame seeds, toasted
1 tsp sesame oil
1 tbsp caster sugar
1 tbsp light soy sauce
1 tbsp gochugaru (Korean chilli flakes)
  or 2 tsp red chilli flakes
1 tbsp rice vinegar

Slice the cucumbers 1 cm (½ inch) thick.
   In a mortar and pestle, roughly crush the sesame seeds. Mix the cucumbers with the seeds and other ingredients in a bowl. Serve immediately.

CHINESE SMACKED CUCUMBERS

SERVES 4
PREP 5 MINUTES

This quick Sichuan pickle is perfect served alongside grilled meat, roast pork or a stir-fry.

3 baby cucumbers
3 tsp finely chopped garlic
1 tbsp caster sugar
1 tbsp light soy sauce
1 tbsp black vinegar
1 tbsp roasted chilli flakes in oil

Using a small rolling pin, smack the cucumbers so they break into pieces. Alternatively, slice in half lengthways and then rip into pieces with your hands.
   In a medium bowl, mix together the remaining ingredients and toss gently with the cucumbers. Serve within an hour or so of making.

PICKLED RED CHILLI AND SHALLOTS

SERVES 4
PREP 5 MINUTES, PLUS 1 HOUR STANDING

I particularly like these chillies and shallots added to South East Asian soups or stews.

2 long red chillies, sliced
6 small shallots, quartered
45 ml (1½ fl oz) rice vinegar
1 tsp sea salt
1 tsp caster sugar

Place all the ingredients in a small bowl and mix well to dissolve the sugar and salt. Leave to sit for 1 hour before using. If you have any leftover, store in a glass jar with a fitted lid and refrigerate for up to a week.

GINGER PICKLES

SERVES 4
PREP 5 MINUTES, PLUS 30 MINUTES SALTING
AND 3 HOURS MARINATING

A little pickled element is an essential condiment for practically any Asian meal. If you want tasty pickles that don't need days to cure, then this is a quick fix. The red chilli is optional if you like a bit of extra heat.

300 g (10½ oz) baby cucumbers
1 tbsp sea salt
2 tsp light soy sauce
75 ml (2½ fl oz) rice vinegar
3 tbsp caster sugar
3 cm (1¼ inch) ginger, julienned
1 thumb-sized red chilli, sliced (optional)

Slice the cucumbers 2 cm (¾ inch) thick, place in a sieve and toss with the salt. Leave for 30 minutes, rinse and dry well on a tea towel.

Add the remaining ingredients to a plastic container with a fitted lid. Toss the cucumbers in the mixture, cover and refrigerate for at least 3 hours before eating.

QUICK KIMCHEE

MAKES 500 G (1 LB 2 OZ) KIMCHEE
PREP 15 MINUTES, PLUS 1 HOUR SALTING
AND 1 DAY MARINATING

In Korea they sell small refrigerators to store your kimchee, so the lingering odours don't overpower your kitchen. This fresh version uses fish sauce in place of the little prawns that usually help kimchee ferment – it is therefore less 'funky' smelling.

1 small Chinese cabbage (wong bok or Napa)
    (700 g/1 lb 9 oz after trimming)
2 tbsp sea salt
10 garlic cloves
5 cm (2 inch) piece pineapple, pear or apple
5 cm (2 inch) ginger
75 g (2½ oz) caster sugar
1½ tbsp fish sauce
1½ tbsp light soy sauce
30 g (1 oz) gochugaru (Korean chilli flakes)
150 g (5 oz) carrots, julienned

Halve and core the cabbage, then cut into 6 cm (2½ inch) chunky pieces. Place in a large bowl with 1 litre (34 fl oz) water and the sea salt. Leave for 1 hour or cover and refrigerate overnight if time permits. Rinse and drain the cabbage.

In a food processor, purée the garlic, fruit, ginger, sugar, fish sauce, soy sauce, chilli flakes and 2 tablespoons of water. Place the drained cabbage and carrots in a sealable container and pour the mixture over the top. Mix it with your hands so you get the sauce into all the wrinkles of the cabbage

Refrigerate for at least 24 hours and up to 2 weeks. After 1 day you can eat, but the flavours will become stronger each day.

Malay cuisine is a mash-up of local Chinese, Thai and Indian influences, which makes their soups, curries and noodles dazzle with exotic spices, creamy coconut and hot chillies. What distinguishes laksa paste from red curry is the use of nuts. Traditionally it's candlenuts, but they're tricky to source so I use macadamias.

PRAWN LAKSA

**SERVES 4 AS A STARTER
OR 2 LARGE PORTIONS**

**PREP 15 MINUTES
COOK 20 MINUTES**

6 macadamia nuts
1 tbsp vegetable oil
75 g (2½ oz) yellow or red
    curry paste
250 ml (8½ fl oz) chicken stock
1 x 400 g (14 oz) tin coconut milk
2 whole star anise
2 cinnamon sticks
3 tbsp tamarind purée
2 tbsp palm sugar
2 tbsp fish sauce
2 tbsp lime juice
150 g (5 oz) green beans, chopped
200 g (7 oz) large raw prawns
200 g (7 oz) thin rice vermicelli
100 g (3½ oz) pineapple
large handful each chopped
    coriander (cilantro) and
    mint leaves

Pickled red chilli and shallots
    (see page 52) and crispy fried
    shallots, to serve

Using a mortar and pestle, crush the macadamia nuts to a fine paste.

In a large saucepan, heat the vegetable oil and add the curry paste and crushed macadamia nuts. Turn the heat down to medium and cook for 5 minutes. Pour in the stock, coconut milk, spices, tamarind, palm sugar, fish sauce and lime juice. Bring to a simmer and cook for 10 minutes, then add the beans and prawns. Simmer for 2–3 minutes and remove from the heat.

Pour boiling water over the rice noodles and leave for 2 minutes or until soft.

Cut the pineapple into 2 cm (¾ inch) batons.

Divide the noodles among four large bowls and ladle the laksa over. Top with the pineapple, chopped coriander and mint and pickled red chilli and shallots. Serve with crispy fried shallots.

NOTE

The taste of this soup relies on using good stock, so it is worth making the Master Asian chicken stock (see page 77). If you're short on time, make the stock in a pressure cooker. It takes about 30 minutes and you end up with stock that would normally require at least 2 hours to cook. You can also use a good-quality bought chicken stock.

You can use a pressure cooker to speed up the cooking of this iconic Taiwanese dish or make it on the weekend when you can putter around the kitchen and take in all the lovely smells. Toban jiang, the fermented broad bean paste, adds a spicy, salty kick and is worth seeking out. Buy it online or visit your local Asian store.

TAIWANESE BEEF NOODLE SOUP

SERVES 4
PREP 20 MINUTES
COOK 2 HOURS

2 tbsp vegetable oil
900 g (2 lb) beef shin
5 garlic cloves, sliced
2 onions, quartered
4 cm (1½ inch) ginger, chopped
1 tsp Sichuan peppercorns
1 tsp fennel seeds
3 whole star anise
1 tbsp red chilli flakes
2 tbsp toban jiang
   (hot chilli bean paste)
1 tbsp black vinegar
1 tbsp soft brown sugar
4 tomatoes, cut in chunks
125 ml (4½ fl oz) light soy sauce
125 ml (4½ fl oz) Shaoxing rice wine
250 g (9 oz) Chinese egg noodles
4 baby bok choy, halved, or Chinese
   broccoli (gai larn), cut in chunks

chopped spring onions
   (scallions), to serve

Add the vegetable oil to a large pan with a fitted lid. Slice the beef shin into 4 cm (1½ inch) pieces. Brown the meat pieces and then add the garlic, onion and ginger and let soften for 5 minutes.

Roughly grind the peppercorns and fennel seeds, then add to the meat with the star anise, chilli flakes, hot bean paste, black vinegar, soft brown sugar, tomatoes, soy and rice wine. Pour about 1 litre (34 fl oz) water into the pan so that the meat is covered by about 3 cm (1¼ inches) of water.

Place the lid on and let the soup simmer for 1 hour 30 minutes or up to 2 hours on the lowest heat possible. Stir every 20–30 minutes so that it doesn't stick. When the meat is fall-apart tender, it's done. Alternatively, you can place everything at this point in a pressure cooker and cook on high for 30 minutes. The opposite can be done with a slow cooker – cook on the low setting for 8 hours or the high setting for 4 hours. Your oven can be used too – cook in a preheated 170°C (325°F) or 150°C (300°F) fan forced oven for 2 hours.

Boil the noodles until al dente, adding the greens in the last minute. Drain and place in four bowls.

Pour the stock/sauce over and top with the meat. Sprinkle the spring onions over to serve.

When you first arrive in hot, humid Vietnam, soup isn't your immediate craving. However, you quickly get initiated into the classics, such as pho and, oddly, they do refresh you. This is loosely based on canh chua tom, which is not dissimilar to tom yum. I've used meatballs instead of prawns, but do use either. Traditionally it's served with the rice alongside, but I like to spoon a dollop into my bowl.

SOUR PORK MEATBALL and RICE SOUP with PINEAPPLE and CRISPY GARLIC

SERVES 4
PREP 10 MINUTES
COOK 20 MINUTES

250 g (9 oz) jasmine or basmati rice
4 lemongrass stems
2 tbsp vegetable oil
4 garlic cloves, thinly sliced
3 cm (1¼ inch) ginger, julienned
2 tbsp tamarind purée
45 ml (1½ fl oz) fish sauce
1 tbsp palm or soft brown sugar
4 ripe tomatoes, seeded, diced
250 g (9 oz) small pork meatballs
   (see note)
700 ml (24 fl oz) chicken stock
5 lime leaves (optional)
200 g (7 oz) pineapple
small handful dill, coriander
   (cilantro) and Thai basil leaves
1 thumb-sized red chilli, thinly sliced

lime wedges, to serve

Boil the rice for about 8 minutes until al dente, drain, rinse in cold water and set aside.

Meanwhile, chop the tough ends off the lemongrass and bash with a rolling pin. Remove the outer layers and set aside.

Heat the vegetable oil and garlic together to slowly let the garlic cook until golden. Keep the heat low so they don't burn, then remove from the pan. Drain on paper towels and set aside.

Add the ginger and whole lemongrass to the pan and let sauté for 3–4 minutes. Add the tamarind, fish sauce and sugar and heat through until the sugar melts. Pour in the tomatoes, uncooked meatballs and stock. Simmer for 10 minutes over a medium heat.

Just before eating, add the lime leaves (if using) and the pineapple cut into 3 cm (1¼ inch cubes) to the stock. Cook for 3 minutes until warmed through.

Serve the soup in four bowls with a big spoonful of rice and the crisp garlic spooned over. Top with the fresh herbs and chilli and serve with lime wedges.

NOTES

The taste of this soup relies on using good stock, so it is worth making the Master Asian chicken stock (see page 77). If you're short on time, make the stock in a pressure cooker. It takes about 30 minutes and you end up with stock that would normally require at least 2 hours to cook. You can also use a good-quality bought chicken or seafood stock.

Use the meatballs recipe on page 178, but substitute pork for the chicken in the recipe.

Hanoi is the spiritual home of pho. Practically every street is dotted with restaurants or stalls solely serving this soup spectacular. Beef pho is the most popular, but it does take a fair amount of time to make. Chicken pho is speedier to pull together and tastes fresher. If you have a pressure cooker, it's even faster. Serve in big bowls with all the fixings – herbs, sriracha, lime and pickles.

CHICKEN PHO

SERVES 4
PREP 20 MINUTES
COOK 45 MINUTES

1 litre (34 fl oz) Master Asian
   chicken stock (see
   page 77 and note)
1 tsp sea salt
5 cm (2 inch) ginger, unpeeled,
   halved lengthways
1 onion, unpeeled, halved
1 cinnamon stick
3 star anise
6 whole cloves
60 ml (2 fl oz) fish sauce
2 tbsp palm sugar
250 g (9 oz) rice noodles
2 large handfuls bean sprouts
large handful each Thai basil,
   coriander (cilantro) and mint
Pickled red chilli and shallots
   (see page 52)

sriracha or other hot chilli sauce
   and lime wedges, to serve

Sieve the chicken stock into a large saucepan and reserve all of the meat from the legs. Discard all of the remaining solids and bones. Heat the stock to a simmer and add the salt.

Preheat your oven grill. Place the ginger and onion on a foil-covered baking tray. Blacken under the grill for 7–10 minutes until the surfaces are quite charred. Add the ginger and onion to the stock along with the cinnamon, star anise, cloves, fish sauce and palm sugar. Simmer for 30 minutes for the flavours to meld. Use a fine sieve to strain out the onion, ginger and spices.

Bring a pan of water to the boil and add the rice noodles. Cook for 1 minute, then drain and arrange in four large bowls.

Add the chicken meat to the bowls and ladle in the broth. Top with the bean sprouts, fresh herbs and some of the chilli and shallots. Pass the sriracha and lime wedges around when serving.

NOTE

Make the chicken stock using 4 chicken leg quarters and without adding the dried mushrooms or optional kombu seaweed. You can also use a good-quality bought chicken stock and cook the chicken leg quarters in that.

Every region of Japan has its archetypal ramen. Sapporo in northern Hokkaido is renowned for its spicy miso ramen, while Fukuoka in the south has its legendary tonkotsu pork bone ramen. If you're going to make ramen for the first time, shoyu is the easiest. Based on chicken broth with roasted pork (chashu), it's easier than making a 24-hour pork broth and having your house smell like a wet soup kitchen.

SHOYU RAMEN *with* PORK, SOFT-BOILED EGG *and* GREENS

SERVES 4
PREP 30 MINUTES
COOK 2–4 HOURS

1 tbsp vegetable oil
900 g (2 lb) rindless rolled
    pork belly
1 litre (34 fl oz) chicken stock
2 eggs
250 g (9 oz) dried ramen noodles
    or 400 g (14 oz) fresh
2 large handfuls chopped greens
75 g (2½ oz) bamboo shoots
4 spring onions (scallions),
    finely chopped

SHOYU TARE SEASONING
1 slice bacon
2 slices ginger
1 tbsp mirin
1 tbsp sake
60 ml (2 fl oz) Japanese
    light soy sauce

togarashi spice mix, toasted sesame
    seeds, nori squares, seared
    shishito/padron peppers, dollop
    yuzu kosho or yuzu or lime juice,
    to serve (optional)

In a large frying pan, heat the vegetable oil. Season the pork with sea salt and freshly ground black pepper and brown on all sides.

Put the stock in a large saucepan, add the pork and poach in the slow-simmering stock for 1½–2 hours. Check with a knife that the pork is done – it will be tender and soft when pierced. Rest it on a plate and cover with foil to keep warm.

While the meat is cooking, make the shoyu tare seasoning. In a small saucepan, heat the bacon and ginger. Sauté until crisp and then pour in the remaining ingredients. Let simmer for 5 minutes and then remove the bacon and ginger. Set aside.

Bring a pan of water to the boil, add the eggs and boil for 6 minutes, then remove and set in iced water to cool.

Reheat the stock and simmer over a very low heat to stay hot.

Boil the noodles for 3–4 minutes until al dente. Keep stirring so they don't stick together. In the last minute, add the greens. Drain and divide among four bowls.

Slice the pork and add two or three pieces to each bowl with the shoyu tare seasoning. Pour the broth into the bowls and add the bamboo shoots. Peel the eggs, slice in half lengthways and place into each bowl along with the spring onions.

Serve immediately with togarashi, sesame seeds, nori, peppers, yuzu kosho or yuzu or lime juice to sprinkle over the top.

NOTE

The taste of this soup relies on using good stock, so it is worth making the Master Asian chicken stock (see page 77). If you're short on time, make the stock in a pressure cooker. It takes about 30 minutes and you end up with stock that would normally require at least 2 hours to cook. You can also use a good-quality bought chicken stock.

RAMENOLOGY

1

Pick your stock base ...
PORK, CHICKEN, FISH, VEGGIE

+

2

Choose your tare flavouring ...
SHIO (SALT), SHORYU (SOY), MISO

+

3

Add cooked ramen noodles ...
FRESH, FROZEN OR DRIED

4

Put in the protein ...
PORK BELLY, CHICKEN, MINCED
PORK, SOFT-BOILED EGG,
PRAWNS, CRAB, FISH CAKE

+

5

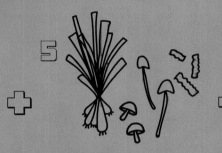

Top it off with ...
CHOPPED NORI, SPRING ONION
(SCALLION), BAMBOO SHOOTS,
SPINACH, GREENS, SAVOY
CABBAGE, BOK CHOY, PICKLED
SHIITAKES, PICKLED CHILLIES

+

6

Sprinkle with a bit of ...
CHILLI PASTE, SESAME SEEDS,
FURIKAKE SPICE MIX,
TOGARASHI SPICE MIX

 BIG DELICIOUS BOWL OF *RAMEN*

RAMEN ETIQUETTE

Hunch over the bowl
when eating.

Use a spoon and
chopsticks to eat
noodles first.

Slurp loudly.

Drink broth last –
straight out of the bowl!

This ramen is based on a Sichuan dish called dan dan noodles. It uses ground sesame seeds, chilli paste and a host of other tasty soy-based elements. Traditionally minced pork is added, but I like chicken thighs. You can mince them in your food processor and it makes a light change from the red meat version.

TANTANMEN SPICY MISO CHICKEN RAMEN

SERVES 4
PREP 10 MINUTES
COOK 20 MINUTES

1 litre (34 fl oz) chicken stock
250 g (9 oz) boneless skinless
   chicken thighs
1 tbsp sesame oil
2 garlic cloves, finely chopped
3 cm (1¼ inch) ginger, chopped
1 tbsp sesame seeds, toasted
3 tbsp miso
60 ml (2 fl oz) mirin
2 tbsp Japanese light soy sauce
1 tbsp hot chilli sauce
200 g (7 oz) greens, chopped
2 eggs
250 g (9 oz) dried ramen noodles or
   400 g (14 oz) fresh
40 g (1½ oz) bamboo shoots

nori strips, furikake spice mix,
   toasted sesame seeds, yuzu or
   lime juice, to serve (optional)

Heat the stock in a saucepan and keep at a low simmer.

In a food processor, pulse the chicken thighs until they are finely minced.

In a large frying pan, heat the sesame oil. Add the garlic and ginger and sauté for 4 minutes until golden. Add the chicken and cooked until browned, about 5 minutes.

Finely grind the sesame seeds, then add to a small bowl and whisk together with the miso, mirin, soy sauce and chilli paste. Pour over the chicken, toss together and then set aside.

Bring a large pan of water to the boil and add the greens. Boil for 30 seconds and scoop out. Rinse under cold water and set aside. Add the eggs to the boiling water. Boil for 6 minutes and then remove and set in iced water to cool.

Add the noodles to the same pan and cook for 3–4 minutes until al dente, stirring so they don't stick together. Drain and divide among four bowls. Place the greens in the bowls.

Add the chicken and chilli miso sauce to each bowl. Pour the broth over each one and add the bamboo shoots. Peel the eggs, slice in half lengthways and place into each bowl.

Serve with your choice of toppings, like nori strips, furikake, sesame seeds and yuzu or lime juice, to sprinkle over the top.

NOTE

The taste of this soup relies on using good stock, so it is worth making the Master Asian chicken stock (see page 77). If you're short on time, make the stock in a pressure cooker. It takes about 30 minutes and you end up with stock that would normally require at least 2 hours to cook. You can also use a good-quality bought chicken stock.

Broth is vital to ramen – it's the soul of the bowl and if you don't get that right, it doesn't work. Although I love chicken stock, it's good to have a vegetarian one as well. Too often they lack oomph, but get a few dried shiitakes, roasted veg and kombu involved and your umami factor rises quickly. The other important element is the tare seasoning, made here with chilli, miso and citrus.

VEGETARIAN RAMEN *with* BABY CORN *and* PICKLED SHIITAKES

SERVES 4
PREP 15 MINUTES
COOK 15 MINUTES

1.2 litres (40 fl oz) Vegetarian mushroom stock (see page 78)
2 tbsp rice vinegar
150 g (5 oz) tenderstem broccoli
2 eggs
100 g (3½ oz) baby corn, blanched
250 g (9 oz) dried ramen noodles or 400 g (14 oz) fresh
2 large carrots, julienned
75 g (2½ oz) bamboo shoots
4 spring onions (scallions), chopped

MISO CHILLI TARE SEASONING
60 ml (2 fl oz) mirin
45 ml (1½ fl oz) sake
100 g (3½ oz) miso
1 tbsp yuzu or lime juice
2 garlic cloves, grated
2 tsp sriracha or other hot chilli sauce
1 tsp grated ginger

togarashi spice mix, nori squares, dollop yuzu kosho or yuzu or lime juice, to serve (optional)

Prepare the vegetarian stock, fishing out the shiitake mushrooms from the vegetables before discarding the solids. Slice them and place in a small bowl with the rice vinegar and a sprinkle of salt.

In a small bowl, mix together all the miso chilli tare seasoning ingredients and set aside.

Chop the broccoli into 5–7.5 cm (2–3 inch) pieces.

Bring a pan of water to the boil and add the eggs. Boil for 6 minutes and then remove and leave in iced water to cool. Peel and set aside. Use the same boiling water to blanch the baby corn and broccoli for 1 minute. Drain and rinse in cold water.

Heat the stock and bring back to a boil. Whisk in the miso chilli tare seasoning.

Boil the noodles for about 3 minutes until al dente, stirring so they don't stick together. Drain and divide among four bowls. Pour the stock over each bowl.

Add some broccoli, baby corn, carrot, bamboo shoots, half an egg and the mushrooms.

Serve with your choice of toppings, like togarashi, nori paper and yuzu kosho or yuzu or lime juice, to sprinkle over the top.

NOTE
Thin alkaline wheat ramen noodles are paramount here – available from Asian stores or online. The added alkaline is what gives the noodles their characteristic chewiness. Avoid packs of pre-cooked ramen or dried square rafts – both are poor quality and too soft.

Making your own udon is no more difficult than making homemade pasta. If you have a standing electric mixer to knead the dough, it makes it particularly easy. Once you've made a batch, it can be refrigerated for later or even frozen. Use in a miso soup, the Yaki udon stir-fry (see page 209) or as a base for the Japanese vegetable miso curry (see page 164).

HOMEMADE UDON NOODLES

MAKES 450 G (1 LB)
**PREP 30 MINUTES, PLUS
3–4 HOURS RESTING**
COOK 5 MINUTES

1 tbsp sea salt
250 ml (8½ fl oz) warm water
450 g (1 lb) '00' fine flour or plain
flour or half of each, plus extra

To make the noodles, first dissolve the salt in the water. Place the flour in the bowl of an electric mixer fitted with a dough hook. With the motor on low speed, add the water and knead for 8–10 minutes or until the dough is soft and smooth. Add a tablespoon more of flour, if necessary, to help the bottom come unstuck if it seems wet.

Alternatively, to make by hand place the flour in a mound on your work surface, make a well in the centre and then pour the water in. Gradually incorporate the flour until the dough comes together, then knead for 8–10 minutes.

Place the dough in a zip lock bag or bowl covered tightly with plastic wrap. Stand at room temperature for 3–4 hours to rest.

To check if the dough is ready to use, make an indentation with your finger. If the dough bounces back, give it another hour and if it stays, it is ready to use. You can also make the dough and leave it covered in the refrigerator for 1 day. Bring back to room temperature before rolling out.

Cut the dough into four pieces. Using a rolling pin, roll out each piece of dough to a 5 mm (¼ inch) thick rectangle. Sprinkle both sides with flour so it doesn't stick.

Using a sharp knife, cut the rectangles into 5 mm (¼ inch) wide strips. Untangle the noodles, grasping 10 or so strands, and then roll into a nest on the floured surface. Sprinkle with more flour.

Keep the noodles covered with a tea towel until ready to cook.

NOTE

To store the noodles, place on trays covered with baking paper. Add a dusting of flour, then another layer of baking paper and finally cover in plastic wrap. The noodles will keep for 1–2 days refrigerated.

Japan's culinary jewels are the restaurants that pay homage to just one type of noodle. My son and I stumbled across a ten-seater restaurant where udon was the rock star. The only dish on the menu was bowls of fat, chewy noodles in a simple stock with crisp tempura. If you don't want to go to the trouble of making the tempura, use sliced duck breast, silken tofu, a soft-boiled egg or cooked pork.

UDON SOUP *WITH* TEMPURA *AND* SPRING ONION

SERVES 4
PREP 20 MINUTES
COOK 30 MINUTES

1 litre (34 fl oz) chicken or
    dashi stock
60 ml (2 fl oz) Japanese soy sauce
60 ml (2 fl oz) mirin
1 tsp caster sugar
300 g (10½ oz) frozen or
    fresh udon (see opposite)
    or 250 g (9 oz) dried
Prawn and sweet onion tempura
    (see page 10) or Agedashi tofu
    (see page 36)
4 spring onions (scallions),
    finely chopped

togarashi spice mix, to serve

Heat the chicken or dashi stock and add the soy, mirin and sugar. Keep to a low simmer.

Boil the water to cook the noodles. Pour in a cup of cold water as the lower temperature helps the thick noodles cook more evenly. If using dry, they will take 6–7 minutes. Fresh will take 4–5 minutes and frozen only 2 minutes as they are partially cooked. Drain, rinse under warm water and let sit while you prepare the other ingredients. Just before serving, run hot water over the noodles to unstick them.

Have four bowls ready to go and the stock simmering. Cook the tempura or tofu as per the recipe. Place the noodles in the four bowls, ladle the stock on top and sprinkle with spring onions, a few pieces of tempura or tofu and a good shake of togarashi.

NOTES

Frozen udon are the best quality unless you make your own. Japanese stores carry them, but usually I use dried. Give the pre-cooked packs, which are sad and mushy, a big miss.

The taste of this soup relies on using good stock, so it is worth making the Master Asian chicken stock (see page 77). If you're short on time, make the stock in a pressure cooker. It takes about 30 minutes and you end up with stock that would normally require at least 2 hours to cook. You can also use good-quality bought chicken stock.

Alternatively, use the Dashi stock (see page 77) or if you want to make a miso version of this soup, just add 3 tablespoons of miso paste to the stock before adding any of the other ingredients.

This much-loved Chinese soup has a special place in my heart. Purported to have restorative qualities, it's just what's needed on a cold winter's day. Black vinegar delivers a zing of sour and white pepper counters it with subtle heat. The vinegar is imperative, so order the Chinese black variety online if you can't find it. I've kept this meat free, but you can add thin pieces of pork for a more substantial soup.

CHINESE HOT-AND-SOUR MUSHROOM SOUP

SERVES 4
PREP 15 MINUTES
COOK 10 MINUTES

8 dried mushrooms
500 ml (17 fl oz) boiling water
1 tbsp sesame oil
3 cm (1¼ inch) ginger, shredded
1 garlic clove, crushed
200 g (7 oz) mushrooms
500 ml (17 fl oz) good-quality stock
100 g (3½ oz) bamboo shoots
1 tsp white peppercorns
2 tbsp light soy sauce
60 ml (2 fl oz) black vinegar
1 egg, beaten
1 tbsp cornflour
150 g (5 oz) silken or firm tofu

handful sliced spring onions
   (scallions), to serve

Soak the dried mushrooms in the boiling water for 15 minutes, then drain, reserving the liquid, and squeeze out the excess water. Discard the stems, then finely chop the caps.

In a large saucepan, heat the sesame oil over a medium–high heat. Sauté the ginger, garlic, dried and fresh mushrooms for 3 minutes or until browned at the edges. Add the stock and mushroom liquid and bring to a boil.

Julienne the bamboo shoots and freshly grind the white peppercorns. Add to the soup with the soy and vinegar.

Beat the egg in a small bowl and pour slowly into the soup.

Mix 1 tablespoon water with the cornflour to make a paste. Pour into the soup and stir until it thickens. Drain the tofu and cut into small cubes. Serve the soup in bowls with a scattering of diced tofu and spring onion.

NOTE

For the mushrooms, use small chestnut or white button mushrooms for the fresh and shiitake or Chinese mushrooms for the dried.

You might need to mop the sweat off your brow when you slurp down a bowl of this 'for-kimchee-lovers-only' Korean soup. Preferably make it with a mild dashi stock as the kimchee packs plenty of assertiveness, although traditionally in Seoul they use an anchovy-based stock, which isn't for the meek hearted. If you have access to good kimchee in a jar, it makes this soup even simpler to prepare.

KIMCHEE AND TOFU SOUP ⟨JJIGAE⟩

SERVES 4
PREP 10 MINUTES
COOK 35 MINUTES

375 g (13 oz) kimchee,
   plus 4 tbsp juices
1 onion, sliced in half moons
1 tbsp light soy sauce
1 tbsp sesame oil
2 tbsp gochujang
   (Korean chilli paste)
1 tbsp gochugaru
   (Korean chilli flakes)
1 tbsp caster sugar
350 ml (9½ fl oz) stock
6 spring onions (scallions), chopped
200 g (7 oz) pork shoulder steak
300 g (10½ oz) silken tofu
10 shiitake mushrooms, sliced

cooked rice, to serve

In a large, heavy saucepan, add the kimchee and its juices, the onion, soy, sesame oil, chilli paste, Korean chilli flakes, sugar, the stock and two-thirds of the spring onion. Cut the pork into thin slices and add to the pan. Place a lid on and let simmer over a low heat for 30 minutes.

Open the lid and give it a stir. Drain the tofu and slice into 2.5 cm (1 inch) pieces. Add the tofu and mushrooms on top of the soup and steam for another 3–4 minutes.

Serve the soup with bowls of warm rice and a sprinkling of the remaining spring onions.

NOTES

You can make the Quick kimchee on page 53 or use a good-quality bought one.

Make the Dashi stock on page 78 or you could also use a good-quality bought chicken or vegetable stock.

This fragrant soup will overwhelm you with intense bursts of lemongrass, lime and seafood. The Thais put A LOT of chilli in theirs and even the fiercest chilli afficionados break out in a sweat. I've kept all the taste, but scaled back on heat. If you can order Thai chilli paste (nam prik pao) online, it's the secret to capturing the quintessential Thai flavour. Alternatively, add two chopped bird's eye chillies.

HOT-AND-SOUR SOUP
with PRAWNS 〈TOM YUM〉

SERVES 4
PREP 20 MINUTES
COOK 40 MINUTES

BASIC STOCK
12 raw prawns with shells/heads on
6 lemongrass stems
3 Thai or other small shallots
3 garlic cloves
20 g (¾ oz) galangal, chopped
1 small bunch coriander (cilantro)
1.5 litres (52 fl oz) chicken stock
8 lime leaves

HOT-AND-SOUR SOUP
3 tbsp Thai chilli paste
200 ml (7 fl oz) coconut milk
4 tbsp lime juice
1 tbsp palm or soft brown sugar
3–4 tbsp fish sauce
200 g (7 oz) baby white
  mushrooms, halved

chopped red chillies, to serve

Peel the prawns and devein, reserving the shells and heads (if you have them).

Finely chop the inner part of the lemongrass. Place the lemongrass, shallots, garlic, galangal and the well washed coriander roots and stems in a mortar and pestle and pound until crushed to a coarse paste. If you don't have a mortar and pestle, place them in a bowl and use the end of a rolling pin.

Transfer the paste to a large saucepan, add the stock, prawn shells and heads and four of the lime leaves. Bring to a simmer over medium heat and cook for 30 minutes. The stock should reduce by one third. Strain the stock through a fine sieve into another saucepan and discard the solids.

To make the hot-and-sour soup, add the chilli paste, coconut milk, lime juice, sugar, fish sauce and mushrooms. Bring to a low simmer and cook for 5 minutes.

Add the prawns and the remaining lime leaves. Simmer for 3–4 minutes or until the mushrooms and prawns are cooked. Ladle into bowls and serve sprinkled with the chopped coriander leaves and red chilli.

NOTE
Traditionally straw mushrooms are used for this soup, but since they are only available in tins, fresh baby white or chestnut or ones keep this soup fresh.

SOUP BUILDING BLOCK BASICS

MASTER ASIAN CHICKEN STOCK

MAKES 1.5 LITRES (52 FL OZ) STOCK
PREP 10 MINUTES
COOK 4 HOURS

Making amazing stock at home isn't a dark art, but it's imperative you start with good ingredients such as free-range chicken. Make a big batch and freeze in doubled-up zip lock bags.

1.3 kg (3 lb) chicken thighs or legs or both
3 large carrots
4 cm (1½ inch) ginger, halved
3 onions, quartered
2 dried shiitake or large dried porcini mushrooms
1 head garlic, halved lengthways
4 celery stalks
1–2 tsp sea salt

Preheat the oven to 200°C (400°F) or 180°C (350°F) fan forced. Place the chicken, carrots, ginger and onion in a large baking tin. Season and roast for 30 minutes. When cooked, pour everything from the tin, including the fat and juices, into a large stockpot.

Add the mushrooms, garlic, celery and 3 litres (100 fl oz) of cold water. Bring to a boil and then turn down to the lowest simmer. Do not stir while the stock is simmering or it will go cloudy. Place a lid on top, leaving a crack open. Let the stock simmer for 3 hours.

Drain everything into a clean pot through a sieve. Reserve the chicken flesh. Skim the excess fat off, leaving some as it adds flavour. Boil for another 30 minutes over medium–high heat to reduce the liquid and concentrate flavour. Add 1–2 teaspoons of salt when it's done, tasting to see if it needs more.

NOTES

To up the umami another level and make chicken dashi, you can add a piece of kombu seaweed to the stock while it's simmering. Before you drain the stock, also add 15 g (½ oz) bonito flakes and leave for 10 minutes to infuse.

Shorten the cooking time by cooking the stock in two batches in a pressure cooker. Alternatively, you can use a slow cooker so you don't have to mind it. Use the slow setting for 8 hours or fast for 4 hours.

DASHI STOCK

MAKES 1 LITRE (35 FL OZ) STOCK
PREP 10 MINUTES
COOK 10 MINUTES

This simple broth is the foundation for so many soups and can be made from start to finish in 15 minutes. Bonito flakes, also known as katsuobushi, are made from skipjack tuna, which is dried, fermented and smoked before being sliced into light-as-a-feather shavings. It adds a smoky, umami dimension that you just can't replicate with any other ingredient. If you don't have a good Asian shop near you, then buy online and get it delivered.

1 large piece kombu seaweed
4 dried shiitake mushrooms (optional – see note)
15 g (½ oz) bonito flakes

Bring 1 litre (35 fl oz) water, the kombu and the shiitake mushrooms, if using, to a boil in a saucepan and simmer for 10 minutes.

Turn off the heat and add the bonito flakes. Leave to steep for 5 minutes and then strain into a clean saucepan.

NOTE

Adding the shiitake mushrooms to the water will give the stock an extra smokiness.

VEGETARIAN MUSHROOM STOCK

MAKES 1.2 LITRES (40 FL OZ) STOCK
PREP 10 MINUTES
COOK 2 HOURS

Roasting the vegetables ahead and adding dried mushrooms bring a rich depth to this veggie broth.

1 leek, cut in chunks
2 large carrots, cut in chunks
4 cm (1½ inch) ginger, sliced
2 onions, quartered
20 g (¾ oz) dried shiitake or porcini mushrooms
1 head garlic, cloves broken apart
1 bunch spring onions (scallions), chopped
2 pieces kombu seaweed
25 g (1 oz) bonito flakes
60 ml (2 fl oz) soy sauce
60 ml (2 fl oz) mirin

Preheat the oven to 200°C (400°F) or 180°C (350°F) fan forced. Place the leek, carrot, ginger and onion in a large baking tin. Season and roast for 30 minutes. When cooked, pour everything from the tin into a large stockpot.

Add the dried mushrooms, garlic, spring onion and kombu. Pour in 2 litres (70 fl oz) water. Bring to the boil and then turn down to the lowest simmer. Place a lid on top and keep almost entirely closed, leaving just a small crack open. Simmer for 1 hour 30 minutes, adding the bonito flakes in the last 5 minutes, and then strain the liquid into a smaller clean pot.

Pour in the soy and mirin, tasting to see if the stock needs additional salt or soy.

MASTER RED CURRY PASTE

MAKES 150 G (5½ OZ) PASTE
PREP 10 MINUTES, PLUS 15 MINUTES SOAKING

This can be used for khao soi gai, laksa or any South East Asian curry. I find Mexican dried chillies work well here because of their size and how easy it is to remove the seeds. You could use large Asian ones, but just double the quantity.

2 New Mexico dried chillies (ancho,
   pasilla or gaujillo)
4 lemongrass stems, inner part only,
   finely chopped
75 g (2½ oz) Thai or other small shallots
5 garlic cloves
20 g (¾ oz) galangal, chopped
½ tsp ground turmeric
1 tbsp shrimp paste or fish sauce
2 Thai or 1 thumb-sized red chilli, seeded
2 lime leaves, finely chopped
1 tbsp chopped coriander (cilantro)
   root or use the stem
2 tsp ground coriander
1 tsp ground cumin

Remove the stems and seeds from the dried chillies. Place in a bowl and pour boiling water over. Leave for 15 minutes or until very soft.

Drain and place the chillies in a blender with all of the remaining ingredients and 90 ml (3 fl oz) water. Blend for about 5 minutes until very fine. Add a little more water if it's difficult to blend.

Scrape the paste into a sterilised jar with a fitted lid and keep refrigerated for up to 30 days. You can also freeze in a zip lock bag with the air pushed out.

CRISP & TOSSED

Miso is the pièce de résistance of Asian salad dressings. Its nutty/salty vibe binds with the citrus, and with a little soy and maple syrup thrown in, the dressing may become your new weekly staple. If eggs aren't your thing, you can replace them with shredded chicken or avocado.

APPLE SALAD WITH A
MISO MAPLE DRESSING

SERVES 4
PREP 15 MINUTES
COOK 10 MINUTES

4 eggs
200 g (7 oz) thin green beans
150 g (5 oz) tenderstem broccoli
100 g (3½ oz) sugar snap peas
1 Granny Smith apple
lemon juice, to coat the apple
2 handfuls pea shoots, wild rocket
   (arugula), baby kale or mizuna
1 tbsp togarashi spice mix

MISO MAPLE DRESSING
30 ml (1 fl oz) light soy sauce
1 tbsp maple syrup
45 ml (1½ fl oz) lime juice
1 tbsp mirin
2 tbsp pale (shiro) miso

Bring a pan of water to a rolling boil. Boil the eggs for 6 minutes (or 7–8 minutes if you like a harder yolk), then immediately place in cold water until cool. Set aside to peel later.

Place all the miso maple dressing ingredients in a small bowl and whisk to combine.

Cook the beans, broccoli and sugar snap peas in a large saucepan of lightly salted boiling water for 1 minute. Drain, rinse under cold running water and drain again. Pat dry on a tea towel and place on a platter. Peel the eggs and cut in half.

Core the unpeeled apple and thinly slice or cut into batons, then coat with the lemon juice to stop it browning. Just before serving, place the vegetables, pea shoots or leaves and apple on a large platter or individual plates. Place the eggs on top. Pour the miso maple dressing over and sprinkle the spice mix over the eggs.

Laab, laap or larb – so many spellings, but they all translate to 'chopped' in this South East Asian specialty. Typically it's pork, chicken or seafood stir-fried and tossed in a sweet-and-sour dressing, but here I've used duck. I like to pad my salad out a bit with carrot and pineapple, but if you don't want to go to the trouble, then leave them out. You can also serve up with thin rice noodles or rice.

DUCK LARB SALAD *WITH* RAINBOW CARROTS *AND* PINEAPPLE

SERVES 4
PREP 20 MINUTES
COOK 10 MINUTES

350 g (12 oz) duck breast meat
1 tbsp fish sauce
2 lemongrass stems, inner part
    only, chopped
1 tbsp vegetable oil
2 lime leaves, finely
    shredded (optional)
3 tsp rice (optional)
2 carrots, julienned
200 g (7 oz) pineapple, chopped
5 Thai shallots, sliced in half moons
1 large handful each coriander
    (cilantro) and mint
    leaves, chopped

LIME GINGER CHILLI DRESSING
2 cm (¾ inch) ginger
1 garlic clove
3 tbsp grated palm sugar or
    soft brown sugar
2 tbsp orange juice
75 ml (2½ fl oz) lime juice
50 ml (2 fl oz) fish sauce
1 Thai or regular red chilli, sliced

crispy fried shallots, to serve
    (optional)

Remove the skin from the duck meat and pulse the meat in a food processor until it's minced. Add the fish sauce and chopped lemongrass and pulse again. In a large frying pan or wok, heat the vegetable oil until very hot. Add the duck and spread it out over the pan. Let it brown well before turning it and grinding over some black pepper. Fry until cooked through and crisp on the edges. Remove from the heat, add the lime leaves, if using, and set aside.

To make the lime ginger chilli dressing, pound the ginger and garlic together with a large mortar and pestle or use the end of a rolling pin in a small bowl. Add the sugar, orange and lime juices, fish sauce and 2 tablespoons water. Mix until the sugar has dissolved. Taste to see if it needs additional sugar or fish sauce, then add the chilli and set aside.

If you're making the toasted rice, place the rice in a small frying pan. Cook for about 3 minutes over medium heat until browned and toasted. Remove from the pan and grind with a mortar and pestle or spice grinder.

Arrange the carrot, pineapple, crispy duck, shallots and the herbs on a platter and pour the dressing over. Sprinkle with the toasted ground rice and crispy fried shallots, if using.

NOTE
You can buy good-quality jars of crispy fried shallots in many Asian shops or supermarkets.

Umeboshi (pickled plums) contain an unusually high level of citric acid and are purported to battle fatigue, eliminate toxins and even aid hangovers. The Japanese eat them for breakfast or with rice. When mashed, they add a lightning bolt of flavour to salad dressings. The plums are sold in jars of paste, but the salted whole plums taste better. Order them online or buy at a Japanese shop.

PRAWN SALAD *WITH* PICKLED PLUM YUZU DRESSING

SERVES 4
PREP 10 MINUTES

100 g (3½ oz) mizuna, wild rocket
   (arugula) or baby kale
180 g (6½ oz) large cooked
   peeled prawns
150 g (5 oz) cherry tomatoes
2 kumquats, thinly sliced (optional)
2 tbsp diced sweet onion
   (see note opposite)
4 red or 1 watermelon radish, sliced

PICKLED PLUM YUZU DRESSING
1 umeboshi (pickled plum)
2 tbsp yuzu juice
1 tbsp Japanese light soy sauce
2 tbsp caster sugar
2 tbsp mirin

To make the pickled plum yuzu dressing, pit the umeboshi and finely chop or mash. In a small bowl, whisk all the ingredients together.
   Place the salad ingredients in a big bowl. Just before serving, toss everything together.

NOTE
Kumquats are a unique fruit with a sweet skin and sour flesh inside. They are optional in this salad so if you can't find them just leave them out or use some slices of peeled mandarin instead.

This carrot dressing is served all over Japan on dense chunks of iceberg lettuce and other vegetables as part of a bento box or as a side salad. It has to be said that once blended, it's not a looker, but have faith because it is tangy, refreshing and insanely good. Sliced tomatoes and crisp sweet onion are the perfect base for its sweet and tart taste.

SLICED TOMATO SALAD *WITH* CARROT GINGER DRESSING

SERVES 4
PREP 10 MINUTES

2 beefsteak tomatoes
300 g (10½ oz) cherry tomatoes
1 small sweet or red onion
10 red radishes
2 large handfuls purple
   micro-cress or purple basil

CARROT GINGER DRESSING
3 tbsp grated carrot
2 tsp grated ginger
2 tbsp chopped onion
1½ tbsp caster sugar
2 tbsp Japanese light soy sauce
2 tbsp rice vinegar
1 tbsp sesame oil
3 tbsp vegetable oil

Place all the carrot ginger dressing ingredients in a blender or food processor (a blender is best for a smoother finish). Blend until the dressing is smooth and pour into a bowl.

Slice the beefsteak tomatoes, halve or quarter the cherry tomatoes and thinly slice the onion and radishes. Arrange all the salad ingredients on a platter and spoon the carrot ginger dressing over to serve.

NOTES
Use the best seasonal or heirloom tomatoes you can find for this simple salad.

Sweet onion works best here – look for varieties such as Vidalia, Maui or Walla Walla.

Soba noodles are best served cold and are the perfect foil for crisp hot salmon and a zesty citrus dressing. You can use any green vegetable with this, such as green beans or tenderstem broccoli.

GRILLED HONEY SOY SALMON with CITRUS SOBA NOODLES

SERVES 4
PREP 10 MINUTES
COOK 15 MINUTES

500 g (1 lb 2 oz) salmon fillet
2 tbsp Japanese light soy sauce
2 tbsp honey
2 seedless or mandarin oranges
250 g (9 oz) dried soba noodles
200 g (7 oz) asparagus, trimmed
1 finger-sized red chilli, thinly sliced
1 tbsp togarashi spice mix
2 handfuls mizuna or
  wild rocket (arugula)

CITRUS DRESSING
zest and juice 1 seedless or
  mandarin orange
1 tbsp Japanese light soy sauce
1 tbsp honey
2 tbsp lime juice
75 ml (2½ fl oz) yuzu juice
2 tsp grated ginger
1 small Thai shallot, finely chopped

Slice the salmon into four pieces. Mix the soy sauce with the honey in a shallow glass dish, then place the salmon, flesh side down, in the marinade.

Mix together all the citrus dressing ingredients.

Slice the peel from the oranges using a knife and then cut into discs. Set aside.

Bring a very large pan of water to a boil. Add a cup of cold water and then the noodles (the cold water helps slow down the cooking time to prevent the noodles from becoming soggy). Cook for about 7 minutes or until al dente. Add the asparagus in the last 30 seconds of cooking. Drain, rinse in cold water and leave to sit in the sieve until the salmon is done.

Heat your oven grill. Place the salmon on a foil-covered baking tray. Grill for 6–8 minutes until crisp at the edges. If your salmon has skin, then remove it after cooking.

Rinse the noodles again, to detangle. Arrange the noodles and asparagus on four plates. Top with the fish and orange slices and pour on the dressing.

Sprinkle with the chilli and spice mix and serve with some salad leaves strewn over the top.

NOTE
If you don't have the togarashi spice mix, substitute with black or white sesame seeds.

This dish has a bit of all the elements you crave in a good salad: crisp, chopped veggies, grilled meat and a punchy dressing. The list of ingredients might seem long, but it takes very little time to throw it all together. If you don't want to make the lotus wafers, you can buy them, replace them with something crunchy like rice crackers or just leave them out.

GRILLED BEEF SALAD *WITH* SESAME MAPLE DRESSING

SERVES 4
**PREP 20 MINUTES, PLUS
2 HOURS MARINATING**
COOK 35 MINUTES

500 g (1 lb 2 oz) bavette, skirt
   or sirloin steak
2 garlic cloves, crushed
2 tbsp light soy sauce
1 tbsp honey
1 tbsp grated ginger
3 tsp vegetable oil
Lotus wafers (see page 44)

SESAME MAPLE DRESSING
60 g (2 oz) sesame seeds
60 ml (2 fl oz) light soy sauce
60 ml (2 fl oz) rice vinegar
2 tbsp maple syrup
2 tsp sesame oil

SALAD
200 g (7 oz) cherry tomatoes
10 large red radishes
6 spring onions (scallions)
2 baby cucumbers
3 large heritage carrots
2 avocados
100 g (3½ oz) watercress, mizuna,
   baby kale or wild rocket (arugula)

Place the steaks in a zip lock bag and add the garlic, soy, honey and ginger. Marinate for 2 hours or up to overnight refrigerated.

To make the sesame maple dressing, place the sesame seeds in a dry frying pan. Turn the heat to the lowest setting and let them slowly turn golden, about 10 minutes. Place in a blender with the remaining dressing ingredients and blend until it's a fine liquid. Scrape into a bowl and set aside.

Heat a chargrill pan or outdoor grill. Brush the steak with the oil and grill on direct heat for 3–4 minutes each side for medium rare. Bavette/skirt steak can vary in thickness so if you have a very fat piece, leave it on the heat a little longer. Once cooked, let the steak rest for 10 minutes under foil. Thinly slice and set aside.

To make the salad, halve the cherry tomatoes, thinly slice the radishes and spring onions and cut the baby cucumbers into coins. Slice the carrots into ribbons using a potato peeler and cut the avocados into 4 cm (1½ inch) cubes. Place all of the salad ingredients into a large bowl and add the beef and lotus wafers.

Pour the sesame maple dressing over the salad and toss together. Arrange on a platter to serve.

When the crumbly yolks of eggs join forces with a sharp salad dressing, it's a good situation. I encountered this fried egg salad in Bangkok and was taken by the combination of the crispy warm egg, cold lettuce and sharp lime and chilli dressing. For very little time and money, you can eat like a king.

THAI FRIED EGG SALAD *WITH* LIME CHILLI DRESSING (YAM KHAI DAO)

SERVES 4
PREP 15 MINUTES
COOK 5 MINUTES

1 butter or soft round lettuce
1 large carrot
5 small shallots
2 small Thai chillies
150 g (5 oz) cherry tomatoes
4 tbsp vegetable oil
4 eggs

LIME CHILLI DRESSING
1 garlic clove
2 tbsp palm or soft brown sugar
45 ml (1½ fl oz) fish sauce
2 tbsp orange juice
75 ml (2½ fl oz) lime juice

chopped coriander (cilantro),
  to serve

To make the lime chilli dressing, crush the garlic with a mortar and pestle. Grind until fine and then add the palm sugar and bash again until the sugar is melted. Add the fish sauce and orange and lime juices and set aside. If you are eating straight away, then add a few of the chilli slices from the salad into the dressing. Wait if it's going to be a while as they can make the dressing very spicy if they sit.

Core the lettuce and separate the leaves. Julienne the carrot, slice the shallots and chillies and halve the cherry tomatoes. Arrange the salad ingredients on four plates or one platter.

In a medium frying pan, heat the oil. Crack the eggs into the pan and cook over a high heat, being careful of the spitting oil. Gently turn over and cook for 1–2 minutes. You want the centre to be slightly soft so don't overcook. Remove, cut the eggs into pieces and set on top of the lettuce. Pour the dressing over each plate and sprinkle with coriander.

Poke is a ridiculously healthy raw fish salad that's tossed in a tangy, spicy dressing with crisp sweet onions and tropical fruit. It originated in Hawaii, which may not be situated in Asia, but does produce world-class Japanese-influenced dishes. Serve as a sophisticated starter on its own or add a spoonful of rice alongside for a main.

SPICY TUNA POKE SALAD

SERVES 4
PREP 20 MINUTES

300 g (10½ oz) ruby red tuna
1 small sweet onion
1 baby cucumber
4 spring onions (scallions),
    green part only
1 mango
8 red or 1 small watermelon radish
1 tbsp togarashi or furikake
    spice mix

POKE DRESSING
2 tbsp Japanese light soy sauce
1 tbsp sesame oil
1 tbsp honey
1 tbsp rice vinegar
1 tbsp yuzu juice

cooked rice sprinkled with togarashi
    or furikake spice mix, to serve

Dice the tuna into 1 cm (½ inch) cubes and place in a bowl.

To make the poke dressing, in a medium bowl mix together the soy, sesame oil, honey, vinegar and yuzu juice.

Dice the sweet onion and cucumber, finely slice the spring onion, chop the mango and julienne the radishes and add them to the tuna. Pour the dressing over the salad. Gently mix together.

Arrange the tuna mixture on four plates, place some of the julienned radishes alongside and then sprinkle with the furikake or togarashi. Serve with cooked rice to pass around.

NOTES
Be sure to buy the loin of the tuna with little marbling. Although tuna is my favourite for poke, other fish like salmon and halibut can be used too.

Sweet onion works best here – look for varieties such as Vidalia, Maui or Walla Walla.

TOFU

SILKEN

Wobbly and delicate –
no need to drain or press.

USE IN

HOT POTS

BRAISES

SOUPS

NOODLES

CAN BE CHILLED AND SERVED
WITH A SOY DRESSING

PRESSED

Rubbery texture, springy and
sometimes smoked with seeds.
No soaking or draining needed.

ADD TO

STIR-FRIES

DUMPLINGS

SALADS

CAN BE GRILLED
OR PAN-FRIED

FIRM/ MEDIUM-FIRM

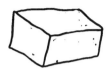

Sold packed in water with a
solid texture. Drain and press.

EXCELLENT FOR

SALADS

RICE BOWLS

FRIED SNACKS

BAO BUNS

SOUPS

CAN BE GRILLED, DEEP FRIED
OR PAN-FRIED

DRAIN AND PRESS

Wrap drained firm tofu in a
tea towel/thick layer of paper
towels. Place a tray on top
and weigh down with tins or
a heavy object. Change the
paper or tea towel a couple
of times until it's dry.

COOK

DEEP FRY

Slice and toss in a
seasoned/spiced
cornflour. Deep fry
in oil in a wok at
180°C (350°F)
until golden
and crisp.

GRILL

Marinate with soy,
chilli sauce, miso
or hoisin. Brush all
sides with oil. Grill
(broil) in the oven,
on a BBQ or
chargrill pan
until marked on
both sides.

STIR-FRY

Brush with oil and
stir-fry in a hot
wok until browned
and crisp.
Combine with
vegetables
and a tasty
stir-fry sauce.

PAN-FRY

Slice and dust with
seasoned/spiced
cornflour. Heat in
a non-stick pan
with 1 tablespoon
of oil until sizzling
hot. Brown all
sides until golden.

Tofu gets a bad rap, but once you find a quality brand and the right type you will be singing its praises. Please have a peruse through my tofu section (see pages 96–97) to get familiar with the different varieties and how to press out the water before cooking. In this salad it is pan-fried until golden and combined with sweet veggies and a citrus soy dressing – it will change the way you think about tofu.

CRISPY SPICED TOFU VEGGIE BOWL with PONZU DRESSING

SERVES 4
PREP 10 MINUTES
COOK 10 MINUTES

400 g (14 oz) firm tofu
4 tbsp togarashi or furikake spice mix
50 g (2 oz) cornflour
100 ml (3½ fl oz) vegetable oil
300 g (10½ oz) tenderstem broccoli
4 kumquats, sliced, seeds removed
2 spring onions (scallions), finely chopped
4 radishes, thinly sliced
2 large handfuls baby kale, mizuna or wild rocket (arugula)

PONZU DRESSING
60 ml (2 fl oz) light soy sauce
60 ml (2 fl oz) yuzu juice
1 tbsp sesame oil
juice 1 lemon
1 tbsp caster sugar
3 tsp finely grated ginger
2 small shallots, finely chopped

Slice the tofu in half and wrap heavily in paper towels or a tea towel. Place a heavy frying pan on top and let the water drain out of it. Change the paper or tea towels a couple of times until the tofu is dry. You will need to repeat this about two times.

Cut the tofu into chunky slices about the size of fat chips (fries). Place the spice mix and the cornflour in a bowl. Mix and then sprinkle all over the tofu until well coated. Set aside.

To make the ponzu dressing, mix together all the dressing ingredients in a small bowl.

Bring a pan of water to the boil for the tenderstem broccoli. Heat a large frying pan with the oil.

When the pan is very hot, cook the pieces of tofu for a minute or so on each side until brown all over, working in batches if necessary.

Blanch the broccoli for 1 minute in the boiling water, drain, then rinse in cold water and drain again.

Place the broccoli in four shallow bowls or plates. Top with the tofu, kumquats, spring onion, radishes and leaves. Pour the dressing over and serve.

If you're preparing anything from the Skewers & Grills chapter (see page 132) or cooking bao buns, then you'll want to make one of these crisp slaws. When making in advance, place the vegetables in ice cold water to keep crisp, then drain and spin before dressing. Choose one of the two dressings.

ASIAN SLAW TWO WAYS – KIMCHEE OR KEWPIE

SERVES 4
PREP 20 MINUTES

200 g (7 oz) white cabbage
3 carrots
1 red onion
1 green chilli
15 red radishes
2 tbsp chopped coriander (cilantro)
2 tbsp sesame seeds, toasted
2 tbsp chopped roasted peanuts

KIMCHEE-STYLE DRESSING
2 tbsp light soy sauce
50 ml (2 fl oz) rice vinegar
1 garlic clove, crushed
1 tbsp honey
1 tbsp sesame oil
1 tbsp fish sauce
2 tbsp gochujang
   (Korean chilli paste)

KEWPIE DRESSING
125 ml (4 fl oz) Kewpie or
   regular mayonnaise
1 tbsp light soy sauce
2 tbsp miso
45 ml (1½ fl oz) rice vinegar
1 tsp hot chilli sauce

Make the dressing of your choice by placing all the ingredients in a screwtop jar with a fitted lid. Shake well and set aside.

Chop the cabbage, julienne the carrots, slice the red onion into half moons and thinly slice the green chilli and radishes. Place all the vegetables, coriander, sesame seeds and peanuts in a bowl and just before serving, toss the slaw with the dressing.

Gado gado, an Indonesian staple, is more of a meal than a salad, and the dressing is the star. The peanuts and soy are blended with tamarind and lime for a salty-sour bonanza. Typically gado gado involves an exhaustive list of ingredients from tofu to cabbage. Mine is a smaller, curated edition that's simple to throw together.

GADO GADO SALAD *WITH* TAMARIND, SOY *AND* PEANUT DRESSING

SERVES 4
PREP 20 MINUTES
COOK 15 MINUTES

250 g (9 oz) baby potatoes
200 g (7 oz) fine green beans
4 small eggs or 8 quail's eggs
75 g (2½ oz) white cabbage
2 baby cucumbers
100 g (3½ oz) cherry tomatoes
2 carrots
4 small shallots

TAMARIND, SOY AND
PEANUT DRESSING
40 g (1½ oz) roasted peanuts
60 ml (2 fl oz) sweet soy sauce
   (kecap manis)
2 tbsp tamarind purée
2 tbsp fish sauce
juice 2 limes
3 tbsp palm sugar
1 garlic clove, finely chopped
1 tbsp sambal oelek chilli sauce

crispy fried shallots, coriander
   (cilantro) and rice crackers,
   to serve

Boil the potatoes in salted water for about 10 minutes until they are tender when you insert a knife. Drain and place back in the pot to dry out.

Boil water in a small saucepan and blanch the green beans for 30 seconds. Drain and rinse in cold water. Pat dry with a tea towel. Soft boil the eggs for 6 minutes (3 minutes for the quail's eggs) and immediately place in cold water to cool. Shred the cabbage, slice the cucumbers, halve the cherry tomatoes, julienne the carrots and thinly slice the shallots.

Place the tamarind, soy and peanut dressing ingredients in a food processor, add 60 ml (2 fl oz) water and blend until fine. Pour into a serving bowl.

Arrange the salad ingredients on a large platter in a composed pattern, creating a section for each item. Peel and half the eggs and place on top.

Pour the dressing over the salad. Serve with crispy fried shallots, coriander and rice crackers.

NOTE

If you don't have sambal oelek, you can substitute another chilli sauce or 1 finely chopped fresh red chilli.

Black rice isn't just coveted for its dramatic beauty; it also possesses a terrific chewiness similar to barley or farro. Unlike rice or quinoa, it has the staying power to sit in a dressing without going soft. The flavours here are drawn from Thai origins, but this is more of a modern mash-up.

BLACK RICE SALAD with PRAWNS and LIME COCONUT DRESSING

SERVES 4
PREP 20 MINUTES
COOK 20 MINUTES

150 g (5½ oz) black rice
1 thumb-sized red chilli, shredded
6 small shallots, sliced
300 g (10½ oz) large cooked
    peeled prawns
60 g (2 oz) coconut flakes, toasted
2 avocados, sliced
2 small mangoes, sliced

LIME COCONUT DRESSING
1 garlic clove
2 cm (¾ inch) ginger
2 tbsp palm sugar
2 tbsp fish sauce
75 ml (2½ fl oz) lime juice,
    plus zest 2 limes
3 tbsp coconut milk

chopped coriander (cilantro),
    to serve

Boil the rice in plenty of water until it's al dente, about 20 minutes. Rinse extremely well in cold water until no more purple water comes out, otherwise it will stain the dressing. Dry on a tea towel to remove any excess water, then add to a large bowl with the chilli and shallot.

To make the lime coconut dressing, with a mortar and pestle grind the garlic and ginger. Add the palm sugar, fish sauce, lime juice and zest and coconut milk. Mix well and pour half the dressing over the rice, tossing until combined.

Add the prawns and coconut flakes and toss again. Pour the salad onto a large platter. Place the avocado and mango slices on top and pour the remaining dressing over just before serving with a sprinkling of coriander.

NOTE
To toast the coconut, bake in an oven preheated to 170°C (325°F) or 150°C (300°F) fan forced for 8 minutes until golden at the edges. You can also use desiccated (grated dried) coconut.

There are many names for this Sichuan specialty, ranging from 'white cut chicken' to 'drool-worthy chicken'. Traditionally it's not a salad, but since it's served at room temperature, it can be taken in a new direction. To bulk it out for dinner, steam some white rice and green vegetables to serve alongside.

MOUTHWATERING WHITE CUT CHICKEN

SERVES 4
PREP 10 MINUTES
COOK 25 MINUTES

500 ml (17 fl oz) chicken stock
4 chicken breasts, with skin
6 spring onions (scallions)
10 red radishes
2 baby cucumbers
2 tbsp chopped roasted peanuts
1 tbsp pickled chillies or sliced
   red chilli
2 tsp sesame seeds, toasted

SICHUAN DRESSING
¼ tsp Sichuan peppercorns, toasted
3 cm (1¼ inch) ginger, grated
2 tbsp roasted chilli flakes
   in oil, drained
1 tbsp toasted sesame oil
3 tbsp light soy sauce
3 tbsp black or rice vinegar
2 tbsp Shaoxing rice wine
1 tbsp caster sugar

coriander (cilantro), to serve

In a medium saucepan, bring the stock to a boil and add the chicken breasts. Boil for 5 minutes, then remove from the heat and place a lid on top of the pan. Leave to sit for 20 minutes, allowing the chicken to cool in the liquid to room temperature.

Julienne the spring onions, then soak in cold water and refrigerate while you make the rest of the salad. This will firm them up and remove the strong onion taste. Quarter or chop the radishes and cut the baby cucumbers into batons.

While the chicken is poaching in the stock, make the Sichuan dressing. Roughly grind the toasted Sichuan peppercorns, then whisk all the ingredients together.

Drain the spring onions and dry on paper towels.

Serve the chicken on a platter or on four plates with the dressing poured over and the radishes, cucumber, spring onions, peanuts, pickled chillies, sesame seeds and fresh coriander scattered over the top.

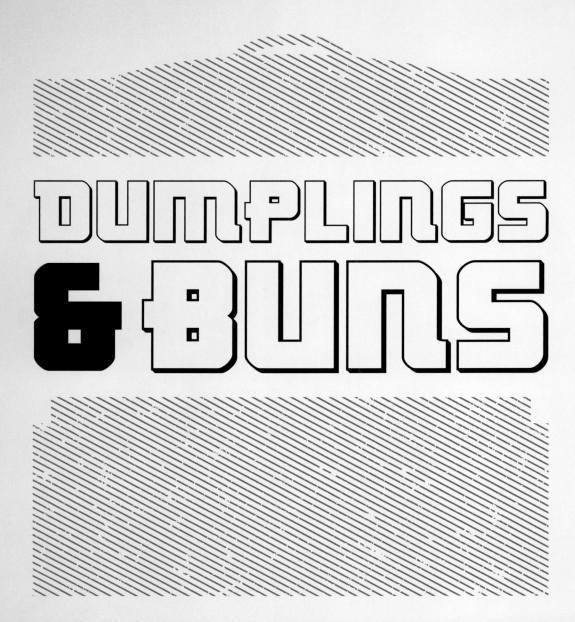

Both the Thais and Chinese serve these open top dumplings. I prefer the Thai rendition as they eat them with fried garlic and sweet soy sauce. Much easier to prepare than gyoza or wontons, shumai can be assembled in moments.

THAI SHUMAI DUMPLINGS

MAKES 20 FAT DUMPLINGS
PREP 30 MINUTES
COOK 8 MINUTES

200 g (7 oz) raw peeled prawns
150 g (5½ oz) minced pork
8 water chestnuts, chopped
1 garlic clove
1 cm (½ inch) slice ginger
small bunch coriander (cilantro)
2 spring onions (scallions), finely
    sliced, plus extra to serve
2 tsp cornflour
1 tsp egg white
2 tsp fish sauce
2 tsp soy sauce
20–25 wonton or gyoza wrappers

FRIED GARLIC
2 tbsp vegetable oil
4 garlic cloves, finely chopped

SWEET SOY DIPPING SAUCE
60 ml (2 fl oz) sweet soy sauce
    (kecap manis)
2 tbsp lime juice
1 thumb-sized red chilli, diced

Roughly chop half of the prawns and place in a bowl with the pork and water chestnuts. Place the garlic and ginger in a food processor and chop until fine, then add the coriander, spring onion and remaining prawns and pulse until chunky. Add the cornflour, egg white, fish and soy sauces and pulse again to mix. Pour into the bowl with the pork and chunky prawns. Mix well and season with freshly ground black pepper.

If using wonton wrappers, snip off the corners of the squares so that they are more round and keep the wrappers covered with a tea towel so that they don't dry out.

Place a wrapper in your hand and spoon 1 heaped tablespoon of the mixture into it. Wrap the wrapper around the filling so that it's pleated round it and the filling comes up nearly to the top. Tap it on the work surface so that the bottom becomes flat and run a knife across the top to smooth over. You want it to be a tight, compact dumpling. Continue with all the wrappers and filling, then place on a plastic tray.

To make the fried garlic, add the oil and garlic to a small frying pan and cook for 1–2 minutes over low heat until golden.

To make the sweet soy dipping sauce, combine all the ingredients in a bowl.

Fill a pot or wok with a couple of inches of water and bring to a boil. Place some baking paper with holes cut through in the bottom of a bamboo steamer. Arrange the dumplings, in batches, so that they are not touching each other, then cover and steam for about 6–8 minutes. Place on a serving dish, scatter with the fried garlic and extra spring onions and serve with the dipping sauce.

NOTE

If you're making the dumplings in advance, arrange on a tray lined with non-stick baking paper. Top with more paper and cover in plastic wrap. Refrigerate for up to 24 hours ahead of steaming. You can also freeze the dumplings raw and steam from frozen.

WONTONS

1

Spoon 1 tablespoon of filling into the middle of a wonton wrapper (use square or round ones).

2

Wet the edges of the wrapper lightly with egg white (hardly any!)

3

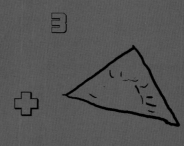

Fold over to form a triangle and press the edges together. Squeeze out any trapped air.

4

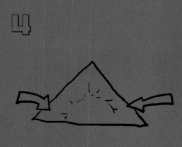

Wet the two farthest corners of the triangle.

5

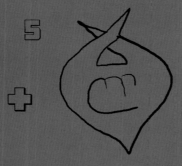

Cross the corners over.

6

Press the two corners together so the wonton sits standing up.

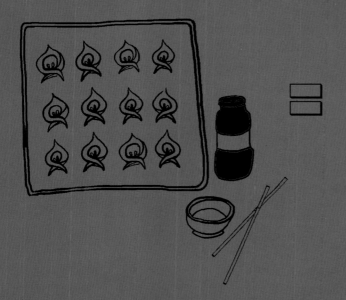

READY FOR THE STEAMER OR SOUP!

It would be a push for me to choose my favourite dumpling, but these are near the top of the list. You can steam or deep fry, but boiling makes them silky soft. Serve in bowls with black vinegar, chilli flakes and soy ladled in. Although you can use any dumpling wrappers (square or round) for these, I find the egg-free type, like gyoza, work best. You can pack more filling in and they are slightly thicker.

PRAWN WONTONS *in a* SPICY SICHUAN SAUCE

MAKES 30–35 WONTONS
PREP 30 MINUTES
COOK 5 MINUTES

1 garlic clove
1.5 cm (⅝ inch) slice ginger
250 g (9 oz) raw peeled prawns
7 water chestnuts
1 tsp light soy sauce
2 spring onions (scallions), green
   and white parts, finely chopped
1 egg white
2 tbsp chopped coriander (cilantro)
30–35 wonton or gyoza wrappers

SPICY SICHUAN SAUCE
1 garlic clove, crushed
1 tsp caster sugar
2 tbsp light soy sauce
1 tbsp roasted chilli flakes
   in oil, drained
2 tbsp black or rice vinegar

toasted sesame seeds and chopped
   spring onions (scallions), to serve

In a food processor, purée the garlic and ginger and then add the prawns, water chestnuts, soy, spring onions, 1 teaspoon of the egg white and the coriander. Keep pulsing, leaving the mixture chunky but together.

Lay out six of the wrappers, keeping the other wrappers covered with a tea towel so that they don't dry out. Place a heaped teaspoon of the filling in each and brush the edges of the wrapper with the remaining egg white. Bring one side over, creating a triangle or half moon. Squeeze out any trapped air. Dab the corners with a little more egg white and cross over, then press them together to form a wonton. Continue until all the wrappers are filled.

To make the spicy Sichuan sauce, mix all the sauce ingredients together and pour into small bowls.

Bring a very large stockpot of water to the boil and have a cup of cold water ready. Add some of the wontons and then add the water. When it comes to the boil again, the wontons are ready to remove. It's best to use a slotted spoon to scoop them out. Drain on a plate. Add the remaining wontons to the water, which should be boiling again. Repeat with the cold water and let cook.

Divide the wontons among the bowls of sauce, top with sesame seeds and chopped spring onions and serve immediately.

BAO

BAO BUNS

1

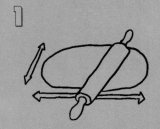

Roll balls of dough into long, oval shapes, 8 cm (3 inches) by 16 cm (6½ inches).

2

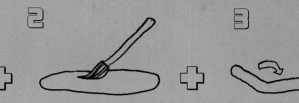

Brush with vegetable oil.

3

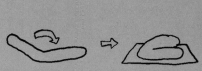

Fold over and place on a square of baking paper.

BAOZi

1

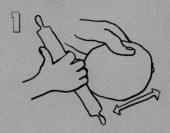

Roll balls of dough into 10 cm (4 inch) circles – thicker in the middle, thinner at the edges.

2

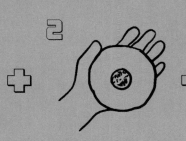

Hold the dough in one hand and place 1 heaped tablespoon of filling into the centre.

3

Add pleats outward in one direction, so the dough 'hugs' the filling as you go round. Use your holding hand thumb to keep the middle open and allow the other thumb to press the pleats.

4

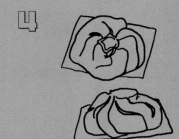

When completed, press the pleats against the hole in the middle and place on a square of baking paper.

=

PAN-FRY AND/OR STEAM TO EAT!

It's taken me years to perfect the fluffiest bao and I can tell you it's the second proving that makes them so soft. If you become addicted, you may want to invest in a big steamer. Asian shops sell aluminium double-stacked steamers, perfect for buns, dumplings or whole fish. Pop in any filling, but Spicy chicken (see page 122), Braised pork (see page 120) or Prawn katsu (see page 118) are memorable feasts.

BAO BUNS

MAKES 12 LARGE BUNS OR 16 SMALLER

PREP 15 MINUTES, PLUS 1 HOUR PROVING

COOK 10 MINUTES

100 ml (3½ fl oz) milk
90 ml (3 fl oz) warm water
2 tbsp vegetable oil, plus extra
1½ tsp fast-action yeast
350 g (12 oz) plain flour
2 tsp baking powder
2 tbsp caster sugar

In a pouring jug, mix together the milk, warm water, vegetable oil and yeast. Leave to sit for 5 minutes to check if the yeast bubbles up (it's a good test to see if your yeast is working).

In the bowl of a standing electric mixer with a dough hook, add the dry ingredients. With the motor running on low speed, pour in the liquid. Let it come together as a ball of dough and if it sticks to the bottom, then sprinkle in an extra tablespoon or so of flour. Knead for 10 minutes on the same low speed. You can also do this by hand using a large mixing bowl and spoon, kneading the dough on the counter for 10 minutes.

Remove the dough and place in a lightly oiled bowl for 1 hour or until doubled in size. Cover with plastic wrap.

Knock the dough back, knead for another 2 minutes, and then cut into 12–16 balls and place under a tea towel to stay soft while rolling. Use scissors to cut 10 cm (4 inch) squares of non-stick baking paper for each ball. Roll each ball into an elliptical shape about 15 cm (6 inches) long and 8 cm (3½ inches) wide. Brush the tops lightly with vegetable oil, fold over and place each on a square of paper. Add to the steamer, then place the lid on the steamer so that they are covered. Leave to rise for a second time, about 30 minutes–1 hour depending on the heat of your kitchen.

Pour water in the bottom of a wok or if you are using a metal steamer, pour water into the bottom of the pan. Bring to a boil and then place the steamer on top. Steam for about 8 minutes or until puffy and firm.

NOTE

If you want to prepare these more than 4–6 hours in advance, I would suggest freezing them cooked and then steaming again from frozen. This keeps them from going stale. You can also store in an airtight container, covered in baking paper, up to a day before using. Once open, they need to be used quickly as they go stale fast.

Never discount the hidden food treasures inside Japan's train stations and airports. There are gems to be found: Michelin-starred restaurants, izakayas and stellar ramen joints. I discovered katsu burgers before catching a flight and was soon salivating over the crisp, panko-coated prawn patties tucked in a bun with chilli mayo and crunchy cabbage. Why not take it a step further with a soft bao?

PRAWN KATSU with SLAW and CHILLI MAYO BAO

MAKES 12 SMALL BURGERS
PREP 20 MINUTES, PLUS
1 HOUR CHILLING
COOK 5 MINUTES

400 g (14 oz) raw peeled prawns
4 spring onions (scallions),
    finely chopped
2 tsp soy sauce
1 tbsp grated ginger
40 g (1½ oz) soft fresh breadcrumbs
2 eggs, whisked
50 g (2 oz) plain flour
100 g (3½ oz) panko breadcrumbs
vegetable oil, for frying
steamed Bao buns (see page 116)

CABBAGE SLAW
2 handfuls finely shredded cabbage
8 red or 1 watermelon radish,
    thinly sliced
1 tbsp rice vinegar

CHILLI MAYO
1 tbsp hot chilli sauce
1 tsp lime juice
1 tbsp mayonnaise
2 tsp sesame seeds

First make the cabbage slaw. In a bowl, combine the cabbage, radishes and vinegar. Add some sea salt and toss together.

To a food processor add half the prawns, the spring onion, soy and ginger and pulse until puréed. Roughly chop the remaining prawns and add to the mixture along with the fresh breadcrumbs. Form into 12 burgers.

Place the eggs, flour and panko breadcrumbs, crushed until fine, in three separate shallow dishes. Dip the burgers into the flour, then egg, then cover in panko breadcrumbs. Repeat with all the burgers. Place on a plate covered with baking paper, cover with more paper and then wrap in plastic wrap. Refrigerate until frying (I find they stay together better if they have an hour in the refrigerator before you fry them).

Mix all the chilli mayo ingredients together in a small bowl and then set aside.

Heat the oil in a wok or deep medium saucepan until it reaches 180–190°C (350–375°F) or when a small piece of bread instantly sizzles. Have a wire rack set on top of a baking tray to drain the burgers, then fry them four or five at a time for about 2–3 minutes until they turn golden.

Serve the bao buns stuffed with the katsu, some chilli mayo and the cabbage slaw.

You can either serve this tender, soft pork belly straight from the slow cooker, roasting tin or pot or pan-fry the chilled thick slices until crisp. Combined with the crushed peanuts, chilli hoisin sauce and pickles, it's ridiculously good.

BRAISED PORK BELLY *with* SPRING ONIONS *and* CRUSHED PEANUTS BAO

SERVES 4
PREP 10 MINUTES
COOK 2 HOURS

2 tsp vegetable oil
2 kg (4 lb 8 oz) skinless pork belly
2 tsp five-spice powder
3 garlic cloves, sliced
100 ml (3½ fl oz) Shaoxing rice wine
60 ml (2 fl oz) light soy sauce
3 cm (1¼ inch) ginger, julienned
2 tbsp soft brown sugar
1 tbsp hoisin sauce
steamed Bao buns (see page 116)

CHILLI HOISIN SAUCE
1 tbsp hot chilli sauce
2 tbsp hoisin sauce

CRUSHED PEANUTS
50 g (2 oz) salted roasted
   peanuts, crushed
1 tsp mild chilli powder

julienned spring onions (scallions)
   and Ginger pickles (see page 53)
   or bought pickles, to serve

In a large frying pan, heat the oil. Season the pork with the five-spice, sea salt and black pepper. Add to the pan and brown on all sides. Remove and place in a slow cooker, large roasting tin or pot.

Add the garlic to the pan and sauté until golden, about 2 minutes. Add all the remaining ingredients, apart from the buns, along with 75 ml (2½ fl oz) water and bring to a boil. Pour the liquid over the meat and cook in the slow cooker on high for 4 hours. Alternatively, you can roast in the roasting tin, covered, at 160°C (315°F) or 140°C (275°F) fan forced for 2½–3 hours or until tender and soft when pierced with a knife.

Mix the chilli sauce ingredients together.

Mix the peanuts and chilli powder together.

Keep the pork belly warm and slice just before serving with the spring onion, peanuts, pickles and the buns.

NOTE

If preparing in advance, chill overnight, arranged in a tray, covered, and weighed down with something heavy to keep it flat. Just before serving, thickly slice the pork and sear it until brown on both sides in a hot frying pan with a little oil.

It's certainly not trad Asian fare, but this much-loved, messy American sandwich, with its sticky sauce of ginger, soy and hoisin, is the perfect partner in crime for bao buns. If you don't have time to make the buns, then just serve the chicken and slaw up in soft brioche or mini burger buns.

SPICY CHICKEN SLOPPY JOE SLIDERS

SERVES 4
PREP 15 MINUTES
COOK 20 MINUTES

2 tbsp vegetable oil
2 celery stalks, diced
1 onion, finely diced
2 garlic cloves, chopped
1 tbsp grated ginger
500 g (1 lb 2 oz) boneless skinless
    chicken thighs, chopped
2 tbsp hot chilli sauce
100 ml (3½ fl oz) hoisin sauce
2 tbsp light soy sauce
2 tbsp rice vinegar
1 tbsp tomato paste
    (concentrated purée)
steamed Bao buns (see page 116)

PICKLED CARROT SLAW
2 carrots, julienned
3 tbsp rice vinegar
1 tsp salt
1 tsp caster sugar

finely chopped green part spring
    onions (scallions), to serve

Place the pickled carrot slaw ingredients in a bowl and mix together. Refrigerate, covered, until serving.

In a large frying pan, heat the vegetable oil. Add the celery, onion, garlic and ginger. Season well and sauté for 10 minutes until soft and golden.

Place the chicken in a food processor. Purée for 1–2 minutes until it is finely minced, When the vegetables are soft, add the chicken and sauté until browned, about 5 minutes.

Add all the remaining ingredients, apart from the buns, along with 2 tablespoons water and cook for about 10 minutes until the sauce thickens.

Just before serving, drain the pickled carrots.

Serve the chicken mixture in the bao buns topped with the carrot slaw and spring onion.

Karaage is a totally addictive fried chicken that's served in izakayas all over Japan. Boneless chicken thighs are marinated in ginger, garlic and soy and then get a dip in cornflour before being fried. It's the perfect counterpart to pillowy bao buns – and the pickles and hot sauce are the icing on the cake, as it were.

FRIED GINGER SOY CHICKEN *WITH* CHILLI SAUCE *AND* PICKLES BAO

MAKES 12 SMALL PIECES
**PREP 10 MINUTES, PLUS
2 HOURS MARINATING**
COOK 5 MINUTES

6 large boneless skinless
    chicken thighs
2 garlic cloves, crushed
2 tbsp Japanese light soy sauce
4 cm (1½ inch) ginger, grated
175 g (6 oz) cornflour
1 tbsp togarashi spice mix
vegetable oil, for frying
steamed Bao buns (see page 116)

CHILLI SAUCE
2 tbsp hot chilli sauce
2 tbsp rice vinegar
1 tbsp caster sugar

Ginger pickles (see page 53) or
    bought pickles, thinly sliced red
    onion and green chilli, coriander
    (cilantro) and lemon wedges,
    to serve

Halve the chicken thighs and place in a bowl with the garlic, soy and ginger and mix well. Cover, refrigerate and ideally leave overnight or for at least 2 hours.

Remove the chicken from the fridge 1 hour before cooking to bring up to room temperature.

Whisk all the chilli sauce ingredients together in a bowl and set aside for serving.

In a shallow dish, mix the cornflour with the spice mix and some sea salt.

Heat the oil in a wok or deep medium saucepan until it reaches 180–190°C (350–375°F) or when a small piece of bread instantly sizzles. Arrange a wire rack over a baking tray ready for draining the fried chicken.

When the oil is ready, dredge the chicken pieces in the flour, shaking off any excess, and drop five or six pieces into the oil. Fry until golden, adjusting the heat so the oil isn't too hot. You want the chicken to fry slowly enough to cook the inside flesh without the crust getting brown too quickly. Drain on the wire rack to keep the outside crisp.

Serve the fried chicken inside the buns with the pickles, red onion, chilli and coriander, with the lemon wedges and chilli sauce to pass around.

One of Taiwan's best street foods, bao dough is stuffed with pork, pan-fried and quickly steamed to cook through. It's the best of all worlds: cloud-like dough, a golden crisp bottom and spicy meat filling. You don't have to do all the fancy pleating (see page 117); the baozi taste good no matter what your folding skills are. Serve with a roasted chilli sauce and, even better, mix in a little black vinegar.

PAN-FRIED and STEAMED BAOZI (SHENG JIAN BAO)

MAKES 16 MEDIUM OR 24 SMALL BUNS

PREP 15 MINUTES, PLUS 1 HOUR PROVING

COOK 10 MINUTES

Bao buns dough (see page 116), made without the oil and baking powder
2 tbsp vegetable oil

PORK FILLING
1 tbsp finely chopped ginger
1 garlic clove, chopped
6 spring onions (scallions), chopped
75 g (2½ oz) savoy cabbage, very finely chopped
300 g (10½ oz) minced pork
2 tsp Shaoxing rice wine
3 tsp soy sauce
2 tsp cornflour, plus extra

black and/or white toasted sesame seeds, finely chopped spring onions (scallions) and roasted chilli flakes in oil, drained, and mixed with black vinegar (optional) or chilli sauce, to serve

Mix and knead the dough as per the Bao buns recipe, but don't add the oil and baking powder. If the dough doesn't straightaway form a ball, add a teaspoon or two of water until it does. After kneading, place in a lightly oiled bowl and cover with plastic wrap. Let double in size. This can take from 1–2 hours, depending on the warmth of your kitchen.

Mix all the ingredients for the pork filling together in a small bowl.

Punch the dough down and knead for 5 minutes. Sprinkle your work surface with a little cornflour. Roll the dough into a long snake and slice into 16 or 24 pieces depending on what you want size wise.

Roll each piece into a circle, about 10 cm (4 inches), and make sure the middle is thicker than the sides. Using scissors, cut 16 or 24 small squares of non-stick baking paper.

Fill each wrapper with a heaped tablespoon of the filling. Start to bring up one side of the wrapper and pleat the outside so that the wrapper stretches around the filling, 'hugging' it. When you finish, press the pleats tightly. They won't always look perfect, but they will taste good! Place each one on a square of baking paper.

Heat the oil in a very large frying pan or two smaller ones with fitted lids (or use a baking sheet that covers the pan). Keeping the heat on medium–low so they don't burn, add the buns, leaving space between them. Pan-fry for 1–2 minutes until lightly crisp on the bottom. Add 40 ml (1¼ fl oz) water to each pan and cover. Cook for 6–8 minutes, removing the lid when the water evaporates. If the buns stick, add a little sesame oil. Crisp the bottoms for another few minutes until dark golden, then remove. Sprinkle with sesame seeds and spring onion and serve with the roasted chilli flakes or sauce.

NOTE
The baozi can be refrigerated for up to 5 hours before cooking. Store on a tray lined with non-stick baking paper and dusted with cornflour. Top with more paper and then wrap in plastic wrap. Bring back to room temperature before cooking.

GYOZA

1

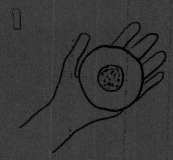

Place 1 tablespoon of filling in the wrapper.

2

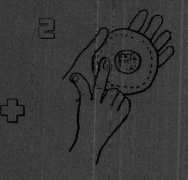

Wet the outer edge of wrapper with water using your finger.

3

Fold over and pinch in the middle with one hand. Place the index finger of your other hand in one side of the wrapper and the thumb outside to begin pleating.

4

Bring a pleat over the front of your thumb, pull your thumb away and press the fold into the back wrapper. Remember that only the front is pleated and pressed towards the back. Make 3 pleats on each side of the wrapper, with the pleats going towards the middle.

5

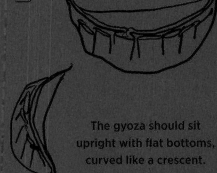

The gyoza should sit upright with flat bottoms, curved like a crescent.

6

ARRANGE IN A HOT OILED PAN IN A CONCENTRIC CIRCLE.

 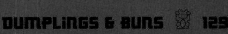

Chinese potstickers and gyoza are not too dissimilar. The concept is the same: the dumplings are pan-fried, quickly steamed and then browned again for a crusty bottom. You can use prawns, minced pork or tofu to replace the chicken. Have a peek at my gyoza folding illustration (see page 129) to get the hang of the pleating. It helps them stand upright in the pan if constructed correctly.

CHICKEN AND SHIITAKE GYOZA WITH MISO LEMON DIPPING SAUCE

MAKES ABOUT 25–30 GYOZA
PREP 45 MINUTES
COOK 5 MINUTES

300 g (10½ oz) boneless skinless chicken thighs, quartered
10 shiitake mushrooms
8 water chestnuts, chopped
3 tsp light soy sauce
2 tsp finely chopped ginger
1 tsp sake or mirin
6 spring onions (scallions), finely chopped
1 tbsp cornflour
25–30 gyoza wrappers
1 tbsp sesame oil

MISO LEMON DIPPING SAUCE
2 tbsp pale (shiro) miso
2 tbsp lemon juice
2 tsp caster sugar
1 tbsp maple syrup
2 tsp sesame seeds, toasted

In a food processor, pulse the chicken thighs until minced, then place in a bowl. Remove the stems from the mushrooms and finely chop, then add to the bowl with the water chestnuts, soy, ginger, sake, spring onion and cornflour. Sprinkle with some freshly ground black pepper and refrigerate until using.

Mix together the miso lemon dipping sauce ingredients and set aside for serving.

Have a bowl of water to hand and a tray lined with non-stick baking paper. Place a wrapper in your hand, floured side down, and place 1 tablespoon of the filling in the middle. Dip your finger in the water and run it lightly around the edge. Pinch the wrapper in the centre to seal the edges together at that spot. Pleat the top of the wrapper from the middle out, pressing it down to the flat edge of the wrapper at the back. Repeat until you have filled all of them.

Heat a large frying pan with a lid over medium–high heat. If you don't have a lid, then use a large baking sheet to sit on top later. Add ½ tablespoon sesame oil. When the pan is starting to get hot, remove from the heat and add the gyoza. Place them in a concentric circle so they hug each other and you are able to get most of them into one pan. When the bottoms become golden after about 2 minutes, add 40 ml (1¼ fl oz) water to the pan. Cover with the lid and cook for 2 minutes until most of the water has evaporated but there is still some left, then take off the lid. Make sure you can move the gyoza around, then drizzle in the rest of the oil around the sides and middle of the pan. Let the bottoms crisp up for 30 seconds more and then remove.

Serve the gyoza with the miso lemon dipping sauce.

NOTE
Buy your wrappers in bulk and freeze them. That way you don't have to scrabble trying to find them on the day you're cooking. To thaw, just leave unopened on the worktop for 1 hour and then place in the refrigerator until ready to use.

SKEWERS & GRILLS

When barbecuing big prawns, the conundrum is whether to take the shells off or not? The shelled ones are much easier for your friends to eat, but they do tend to dry out. I've found that threading a lime leaf over the back of each prawn is a clever way to protect the flesh during grilling and it also infuses an intense lime taste. The coconut marinade keeps the flesh moist and ties in the tropical flavours.

GRILLED COCONUT GINGER PRAWNS *with* PAPAYA SALSA

SERVES 4
PREP 15 MINUTES, PLUS 4 HOURS MARINATING
COOK 5 MINUTES

200 ml (7 fl oz) coconut milk
zest and juice 1 lime
18 lime leaves, 2 finely chopped
1 cm (½ inch) ginger, grated
1 thumb-sized red chilli, sliced
1 tbsp fish sauce
16 very large raw peeled
    prawns with tails

PAPAYA SALSA
1 large or 2 small papayas, diced
½ thumb-sized chilli, chopped
1 tbsp chopped mint

lime wedges, to serve

If using wooden skewers, soak them for 30 minutes before cooking.

In a small bowl, mix together the coconut milk, lime zest and juice, the finely chopped lime leaves, ginger, chilli and fish sauce. Set aside.

Use a sharp knife to slice down the back of each prawn and rinse out the vein.

Thread each prawn with a whole lime leaf on the back onto a wooden or metal skewer. Place in a shallow baking dish and pour half the marinade over. Refrigerate for up to 4 hours before grilling.

To make the papaya salsa, mix the papaya, chilli and mint together in a small bowl and set aside.

Preheat an outdoor grill or chargrill pan. Grill the prawns, lime leaf down, over direct heat for about 3–5 minutes or until they turn pink and are charred at the edges.

Serve the prawns with the remaining marinade, papaya salsa and lime wedges. You could also cook steamed rice to bulk this up.

You can follow your nose to the mu ping stalls at Bangkok's night markets. Bits of marinated pork are skewered, charcoal-grilled and brushed with a coconut and palm sugar glaze. Dipped into a spicy roasted chilli sauce (jaew), it's porcine bliss. A sharp fresh Green papaya salad (see page 198) would make a nice counterpart to the skewers.

PORK SKEWERS ‹mu ping› WITH PALM SUGAR GLAZE and JAEW

SERVES 4
PREP 10 MINUTES, PLUS 2 HOURS MARINATING
COOK 10 MINUTES

4 garlic cloves
2 tsp white peppercorns, crushed
2 tbsp chopped coriander (cilantro) roots or stems
1 tbsp oyster sauce
2 tbsp fish sauce
1 tbsp soy sauce
500 g (1 lb 2 oz) pork shoulder steaks, excess fat trimmed
2 tbsp palm or soft brown sugar
60 ml (2 fl oz) coconut milk
vegetable oil, for brushing

ROASTED CHILLI SAUCE (JAEW)
4 small shallots, sliced in half moons
2 tbsp chopped coriander (cilantro)
60 ml (2 fl oz) fish sauce
75 ml (2½ fl oz) lime juice
1 tbsp palm sugar
1 tbsp red chilli flakes

sliced baby cucumber, shallots and coriander (cilantro), to serve

If using wooden skewers, soak them for 30 minutes before cooking.

To make the marinade, place the garlic, white peppercorns, coriander, oyster, fish and soy sauces in a food processor to blend (alternatively, chop by hand).

Trim the pork of any excess fat and thinly slice the pork about 5 mm (¼ inch) thick. Place in a shallow baking dish or zip lock bag and pour the marinade over. Massage it into the flesh, cover and refrigerate for 2 hours or up to overnight. Remove and bring to room temperature before grilling.

To make the glaze, mix the palm sugar and coconut milk together. Microwave for 1 minute for the sugar to melt or heat in a small saucepan until liquid.

Make the roasted chilli sauce by mixing the ingredients together.

Thread the pork onto the skewers, pushing the meat close together. Preheat your outdoor grill or a chargrill pan. Brush both sides with oil so the meat doesn't stick and crack lots of black pepper over. Grill the skewers over indirect or low heat for 10 minutes. Because pork shoulder is marbled, you want the fat to melt out slowly. Once the meat has browned and is almost done, brush the skewers with the coconut palm glaze on one side and then turn over and repeat on the other side.

Serve the skewers with the roasted chilli sauce, sliced baby cucumbers, shallots and coriander.

NOTE

Pork tenderloin can be used in place of the shoulder steaks or if you can't be bothered to thread the meat onto skewers, you could make an easier version using pork chops or shoulder steaks grilled whole.

Ayam penyet hails from the Indonesian island of Java. Chicken legs are marinated, boiled, smashed and then fried. Sound like a lot of work? Indeed it is, so I've devised a modified version so you can enjoy the same flavours, but with less effort. This is a completely inauthentic preparation, but it captures the essence of the exotic Indonesian flavours – and you'll have fewer dishes to clean up.

INDONESIAN GRILLED CHICKEN LEGS with GREEN and RED SAMBALS

SERVES 4
PREP 30 MINUTES, PLUS
1 HOUR MARINATING
COOK 20 MINUTES

4 lemongrass stems, inner part only
6 garlic cloves
1 small shallot
30 g (1 oz) ginger
1 tsp groud turmeric
1 tsp red chilli flakes
1 tsp ground coriander
60 ml (2 fl oz) light soy sauce
6 large chicken legs with the thighs

GREEN SAMBAL
3 thumb-sized green chillies
3 small shallots, unpeeled, halved
2 garlic cloves, unpeeled
1–2 tbsp fish sauce
1 tbsp caster sugar
20 g (¾ oz) coriander (cilantro)
juice 2 limes

RED SAMBAL
2 tbsp sambal oelek chilli sauce
juice 2 limes
1 tbsp rice vinegar
2 tbsp soft brown sugar
1 small Thai shallot, chopped

chopped shallot and coriander
   (cilantro), to serve

In a food processor, create the marinade by blending together the finely chopped lower third of the lemongrass stems, the garlic, shallot, ginger, turmeric, chilli flakes, ground coriander and soy. Place the chicken in a zip lock bag, pour the marinade over and leave for an hour or up to overnight. Remove and pat dry.

To make the green sambal, in a dry frying pan add the green chillies, shallots and garlic. Cook until blackened on all sides, about 10 minutes. Place the chillies in a plastic bag to steam for 2 minutes. Peel the skins off and remove the seeds. Peel the garlic and shallots and place in a food processor with the chillies. Add the fish sauce, sugar and chopped coriander and pulse to a chunky consistency. Squeeze in the lime juice and taste for additional fish sauce. Scrape into a bowl.

Mix all the red sambal ingredients together in a small bowl and set aside.

Preheat your outdoor grill or chargrill pan. Grill the chicken over indirect low heat for 10 minutes each side until charred at the edges and the skin is starting to pull back.

Serve the grilled chicken with the green and red sambals and garnish with shallots and fresh coriander.

Beef ribs are sold individually and look like small bricks. The bones aren't visible, but once they are slow-cooked a handle appears. The meat can be very tough, so you will need to cook the ribs slowly. Once tenderised, they are ready for a spicy Korean chilli glaze and a quick char on the grill or BBQ.

KOREAN BEEF RIBS WITH A SWEET-AND-SPICY BBQ SAUCE

SERVES 4
PREP 15 MINUTES
COOK 2–4 HOURS, PLUS
10 MINUTES GRILLING

2 tbsp vegetable oil
4 thick beef ribs
6 garlic cloves, peeled
3 cm (1¼ inch) ginger, sliced
60 ml (2 fl oz) light soy sauce
60 ml (2 fl oz) rice or cider vinegar
200 ml (7 fl oz) pineapple juice

PICKLED CARROT
2 large carrots, thinly julienned
2 tbsp rice vinegar
2 tsp caster sugar
2 tsp salt

KOREAN BBQ SAUCE
100 g (3½ oz) gochujang (Korean
   chilli paste) or equal quantities
   miso and sriracha
60 ml (2 fl oz) rice vinegar
30 ml (1 fl oz) mirin
2 tbsp caster sugar
2 tbsp light soy sauce
1 tbsp sesame seeds, toasted

Quick Korean cucumber pickles (see
   page 52), steamed rice and
   lettuce leaves, to serve

Preheat the oven to 160°C (315°F) or 140°C (275°F) fan forced.

In an ovenproof pot with a fitted lid or in a pressure cooker, heat 1 tablespoon of the oil. Brown the meat on all sides and then remove from the pot. Add the garlic and ginger. Sauté over a medium heat for 5 minutes or until very fragrant and golden. Pour in the soy sauce, vinegar and pineapple juice. Bring to a boil and add the ribs.

If using the oven, cover the pot and place in the oven for 2 hours. Check periodically and turn the ribs in the sauce as they cook. You can also use a slow cooker and choose the faster 4 hour setting.

If using the pressure cooker, lock on the lid and cook on high pressure for 30 minutes. Remove from the heat and run under a cold tap until the pressure is released. Check the meat and if it's fork-tender, then it's done. If it's still a little tough, then lock the lid back on and cook for another 10 minutes. Some ribs are bigger than others, so they may need a bit longer.

When the ribs are done, discard the sauce and remove any large pieces of fat. At this point you can refrigerate the meat up to overnight. Remove any solidified pieces of fat once chilled and bring back to room temperature before grilling.

To make the pickled carrot, place the carrot in a bowl and cover with the other ingredients. Toss well and refrigerate until using.

To make the Korean BBQ sauce, whisk all the ingredients together and set aside.

When close to eating, heat an outdoor grill or chargrill pan. Brush the meat with the remaining oil to keep it from sticking. Using direct heat, grill the meat for 10 minutes to warm through. Brush with the BBQ sauce until sticky and the edges are blackened.

Serve the meat with the pickled carrot and cucumbers and the steamed rice and lettuce leaves as well, if you like.

BBQ LiKE A PRO

WHICH IS BETTER - CHARCOAL OR GAS?

ANSWER

CHARCOAL!

- SMOKIER FLAVOUR
- HIGH HEAT
- BEST CHAR

Buy a big and deep BBQ – less flare ups.

Use a charcoal chimney to start coals – no lighter fluid.

Lump hardwood charcoal is best – burns hotter and longer and is cheapest.

Stock up on disposable drip trays for indirect heat.

Clean well with a brush before starting cooking.

Don't turn the meat too much – let it char on one side, then roll over.

Look after your food – don't leave the scene!

Wait for the flames to die down + grill over the glowing coals.

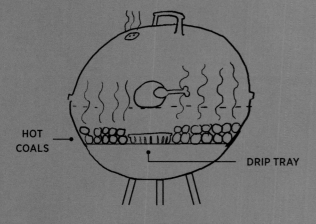

HOT COALS

DRIP TRAY

INDIRECT

LOW AND SLOW

BBQ

RIBS

FATTY SKEWERS
(LIKE PORK BELLY)

CHICKEN WINGS

CHICKEN ON THE BONE

LARGE JOINTS OF MEAT

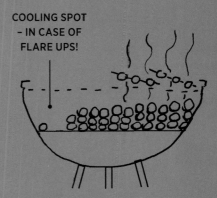

COOLING SPOT
– IN CASE OF
FLARE UPS!

DiRECT

THE PERFECT CHAR

GRiLL

STEAKS

PORK OR BEEF FILLET

YAKITORI OR
SKEWERS

GRILLED VEGETABLES

WHOLE FISH

This is my own version of Japanese BBQ sauce and all of the ingredients are top umami performers. The trick to all great ribs is to slow cook them first and you can do that by either boiling them or cooking them slowly in the oven. Once that's done, they only need a char on the BBQ.

MISO-GLAZED RIBS

SERVES 4
PREP 10 MINUTES
COOK 1 HOUR 15 MINUTES

1 onion, quartered
3 racks pork baby back ribs,
   halved into 6 small racks
150 ml (5 fl oz) tamarind purée
2 garlic cloves, crushed
60 ml (2 fl oz) mirin
60 ml (2 fl oz) rice vinegar
4 tbsp miso
3 tbsp light soy sauce
1 tbsp honey
2 tbsp chilli sauce
2 tbsp sesame seeds, toasted
2 tbsp vegetable oil

chopped coriander (cilantro) and
   sliced green chillies, to serve

Bring a pot of water to a boil. Add the onion and ribs. Boil for 1 hour or for longer, if needed, until the meat is tender. Drain and pat dry.

In a small bowl, mix together the tamarind, garlic, mirin, rice vinegar, miso, soy, honey, chilli sauce and sesame seeds.

Preheat an outdoor grill or chargrill pan. Brush the meat with the oil and season well with sea salt and black pepper. Grill on low direct heat until the edges start to crisp and the meat begins to brown. Start to brush the marinade on and then turn over after 5 minutes. Keep brushing until everything is sticky and golden.

Serve the ribs with a sprinkle of chopped coriander and green chilli and extra marinade to dip into.

NOTE
Choose your favourite chilli sauce to use here. Sriracha, toban jiang or a Chinese chilli sauce are all good.

Tamarind is one of my go-to ingredients for sauces or glazes. It's practically calorie-free and I never tire of its sweet-and-sour vibes. I discovered naam jim jaew, a chilli-garlic tamarind sauce, in Bangkok, where it's served alongside kai yang chicken. It works with any grilled meat or vegetables. Keep the skin on the salmon while it grills as it acts as a barrier and protects the fish from drying out.

GRILLED SALMON WITH STICKY TAMARIND SAUCE

SERVES 4
PREP 10 MINUTES
COOK 15 MINUTES

1 tbsp vegetable oil
4 garlic cloves, finely chopped
200 ml (7 fl oz) tamarind purée
4 tbsp fish sauce
2 tsp red chilli flakes
4 tbsp palm sugar
4 tsp light soy sauce
750 g–850 g (1 lb 10 oz–1 lb 14 oz)
  large salmon fillet, with skin
2 thumb-sized red chillies, shredded
handful mint and coriander
  (cilantro) leaves

steamed rice, to serve

In a small saucepan, heat the oil and slowly sauté the garlic until it goes golden, about 2–3 minutes. Add the tamarind, 100 ml (3½ fl oz) water, the fish sauce, chilli flakes, sugar and soy. Simmer for 5 minutes and then remove from the heat.

Preheat an outdoor grill or chargrill pan. Spoon a couple of tablespoons of the tamarind sauce over the fish and sprinkle over a few chilli slices.

Grill the salmon, skin side down, over low direct heat and with the hood closed if using the outdoor grill, for about 7–8 minutes. It's better if the centre is slightly pink and juicy rather than overcooked. The skin may stick a little to the grill, but don't worry as you will be discarding it anyway.

Peel the skin from the salmon and place the flesh on a platter. Sprinkle with the fresh herbs and remaining red chilli. Serve with the remaining tamarind sauce and steamed rice.

NOTES

Other meaty fish like barramundi, halibut and red snapper would also work nicely here.

Serve this salmon with a refreshing salad of sliced baby cucumbers and small shallots, dressed with a splash of rice wine vinegar and sprinkle of sea salt.

A national dish in Thailand, Singapore and Malaysia, satay is one of the most popular Asian foods in the world. Sadly it is often misinterpreted, with many dried sticks of chicken and bland peanut sauces. I ate this delicious rendition in Bali at a beach BBQ and hopefully it will reaffirm your faith. Chicken thighs are the best meat to use, staying juicy while they turn golden on the charcoal grill.

BEST CHICKEN SATAY (SATAY AYAM)

SERVES 4
PREP 30 MINUTES, PLUS
1 HOUR MARINATING
COOK 20 MINUTES

2 garlic cloves
2 tsp ground coriander
2 tsp ground turmeric
2 tsp mild chilli powder
1 tbsp palm or soft brown sugar
2 tbsp lime juice
2 tbsp sweet soy sauce
   (kecap manis)
400 g (14 oz) boneless skinless
   chicken meat
vegetable oil, for brushing

PEANUT SAUCE
50 g (2 oz) roasted salted peanuts
3 tsp vegetable oil
1 garlic clove, grated
60 ml (2 fl oz) sweet soy (kecap
   manis) or dark soy sauce
2 tbsp tamarind purée
2 tbsp fish sauce
juice 2 limes
3 tbsp palm or soft brown sugar
1 tbsp sambal oelek chilli sauce

chunks baby cucumber and red
   onion wedges, to serve

If using wooden skewers, soak for 30 minutes (no need to worry if using metal).

To make the marinade, blend the garlic, coriander, turmeric, chilli powder, sugar, lime juice and soy together in a food processor.

Cut the chicken into 1 cm (½ inch) or less slices. Place in a shallow ceramic or glass baking dish or zip lock bag. Pour the marinade over the chicken and massage into the meat. Refrigerate for 1 hour or up to overnight. Thread the slices onto the wooden or metal skewers.

To make the peanut sauce, in a food processor purée the roasted peanuts with 60 ml (2 fl oz) water and pulse until very fine.

Heat the oil in a medium saucepan. Add the garlic and cook over a low heat for 2 minutes, stirring often, until golden. Add the remaining peanut sauce ingredients along with the peanuts. If the sauce is too thick, then add a little more water. Sauté over medium heat for 10 minutes and then remove and pour into a serving bowl.

Preheat your outdoor grill or a chargrill pan. Drain the chicken, brush with oil and cook on direct medium heat or, if using charcoal, cook on direct heat when the coals have died down a bit. Grill for 2–3 minutes.

Serve the satay with the peanut sauce, cucumber and onion wedges. You can also add some steamed or sticky rice to bulk it out.

NOTE
If you don't have sambal oelek, you can substitute another chilli sauce or 1 finely chopped fresh red chilli.

Indonesian sweet soy sauce has many uses. Made from fermented black soya beans and palm sugar, it has a hint of star anise and cinnamon. Not just for rice or noodle dishes, it doubles as a dipping sauce and with a little lime or rice vinegar to balance out its sweetness, it also transforms into a stunning zingy dressing.

GRILLED EGGPLANT WITH SWEET SOY AND LIME DRESSING

SERVES 4
PREP 20 MINUTES, PLUS 30 MINUTES CHILLING
COOK 15 MINUTES

3 small–medium eggplants
 (aubergines)
3–4 tbsp vegetable oil
1 thumb-sized red chilli, julienned
1 spring onion (scallion), julienned
3 tbsp roasted peanuts,
 finely chopped
small handful coriander (cilantro)
 leaves, chopped

SWEET SOY AND LIME DRESSING
60 ml (2 fl oz) sweet soy sauce
 (kecap manis)
1 thumb-sized red chilli, chopped
1 garlic clove, finely chopped
2 tsp finely chopped ginger
juice 2 limes
1 tablepoon caster sugar

Thickly slice the eggplants and brush with oil. Lightly score a criss-cross pattern on one side of each with a knife to help them cook faster. Season with sea salt and freshly ground black pepper.

Preheat an outdoor grill or chargrill pan and grill the eggplant until black grill marks appear, about 2 minutes each side. Remove and set on a platter.

Wrap the spring onion and chilli in wet paper towels and refrigerate for 30 minutes to get crisp.

To make the sweet soy and lime dressing, mix all the ingredients together until the sugar is dissolved.

Pour the lime dressing over the eggplant on the platter. Scatter the julienned chilli and spring onion over and top with the chopped peanuts and coriander leaves.

In the outer Chinese border provinces like Xinjiang, near Mongolia, the cuisine starts to mingle with Middle Eastern influences and lamb features prominently. These tasty spice-crusted cutlets originated in this far-flung outpost, but are popular street food all over China. You can also make this as skewers.

SPICE-CRUSTED XINJIANG LAMB *WITH* SMACKED CUCUMBER

SERVES 4
PREP 10 MINUTES, PLUS 30 MINUTES MARINATING
COOK 5 MINUTES

2 racks lamb, French trimmed
2 garlic cloves, crushed
1 tbsp light soy sauce
1 tbsp sesame oil
1 tbsp Shaoxing rice wine
1 tbsp fennel seeds
1 tbsp cumin seeds
1 tbsp Sichuan peppercorns
1 tbsp red chilli flakes
6 baby cucumbers, ends trimmed

SESAME SAUCE
2 garlic cloves, finely crushed
2 tbsp caster sugar
2 tbsp light soy sauce
2 tbsp black or rice vinegar
2 tbsp roasted chilli flakes
   in oil, drained
1 tbsp sesame seeds, toasted

Remove any outer fat from the lamb racks and slice into individual cutlets. In a shallow baking dish, mix togther the garlic, soy, sesame oil and rice wine and massage into the lamb flesh. Leave to marinate for 30 minutes or up to overnight, covered and refrigerated.

Place all the spices, except for the chilli flakes, in a small saucepan. Toast for 1 minute over medium heat and then place in a mortar and pestle. Roughly grind the spices and mix the chilli flakes in. Pour the spices onto a large plate. Dip in each cutlet so that it's covered on both sides. Set aside or refrigerate until ready to grill.

To make the sesame sauce, mix all the ingredients together in a small bowl.

Place the cucumbers on a chopping board. Smack the top of them lightly with a rolling pin. Place the chunky pieces in a bowl, spoon 1–2 tablespoons of the sesame sauce over and mix together. Set aside the remaining sauce to serve with the lamb.

Preheat an outdoor grill or chargrill pan and cook the cutlets for 1–2 minutes each side over direct heat. Serve with the smacked cucumber and the sesame sauce for dipping.

In Takayama, Japan, the mountainous area famous for its sake and Hida beef, I discovered the wonders of grilled beef with miso. Its grass-fed cattle produce the much prized, fat-laced meat and the local restaurants charcoal grill it with lashings of nutty miso and chilli paste. Inspired by such a treat, I decided to try it on other meats like these pork chops. It's a big return for something so simple.

MISO CHILLI PORK CHOPS WITH KUMQUAT MIZUNA SALAD

SERVES 4
**PREP 10 MINUTES, PLUS
30 MINUTES MARINATING**
COOK 10 MINUTES

2 tbsp miso
2 tsp Japanese or other
   light soy sauce
2 tbsp rice vinegar
1 tbsp honey
2 tbsp hot chilli sauce
4 large pork chops with
   bone attached
vegetable oil, for brushing

KUMQUAT MIZUNA SALAD
100 g (3½ oz) mizuna or wild
   rocket (arugula)
1 shallot, very thinly sliced
4 kumquats
2 tsp sesame seeds, toasted
1 tbsp yuzu juice
1 tsp sesame oil

To make the marinade, in a small bowl mix together the miso, soy, rice vinegar, honey and chilli sauce. Spread both sides of the pork with some of the marinade and leave the rest for a dipping sauce. You can marinate the chops for 30 minutes or up to overnight, covered and refrigerated.

To make the kumquat mizuna salad, in a salad bowl mix together the mizuna and shallot. Slice the kumquats in half, remove the flesh and seeds and then finely slice. Add to the salad. Sprinkle over the sesame seeds. Mix the yuzu and sesame oil together in a bowl and save to dress the salad right before eating.

Preheat an outdoor grill or chargrill pan. Drain the pork and brush with oil. Grill the pork for 3–4 minutes each side, depending on the thickness. Remove and let rest under foil for 5 minutes.

Serve the chops with the salad and reserved sauce.

This bulgogi grilled steak taco with chilli mayo and kimchee slaw will make you rethink 'fusion' food. Normally I'm a traditionalist, but this is too delicious to pass up. Roy Choi is the genius creator of this and his Kogi Korean taco trucks in LA spawned a global street food revolution.

KOREAN GRILLED STEAK TACOS *with* KIMCHEE SLAW

SERVES 4
PREP 20 MINUTES, PLUS
30 MINUTES MARINATING
COOK 15 MINUTES

4 garlic cloves
3 cm (1¼ inch) ginger
2 tbsp sesame oil
2 tbsp caster sugar
2 tbsp light soy sauce
1 tbsp gochugaru (Korean
   chilli flakes)
700 g (1 lb 9 oz) ribeye, skirt steak
   or beef kalbi rib steaks
8 corn tortillas
vegetable oil, for brushing

SPICY MAYO
1 tbsp gochujang (Korean chilli
   paste) or sriracha
1 tbsp lime juice
2 tbsp Kewpie or
   regular mayonnaise

½ quantity Kimchee-style slaw
   (see page 100), to serve

To make the spicy mayo, in a small bowl mix all the ingredients together and set aside.

To make the marinade, add the garlic, ginger, sesame oil, sugar, soy sauce and chilli flakes to a food processor and blend until smooth. Pour over the beef and marinate for 30 minutes or up to overnight, refrigerated and covered.

Preheat the oven to 200°C (400°F) or 180°C (350°F) fan forced. Wrap the tortillas in a thin tea towel wrapped in foil and place in the oven to warm through. Alternatively, you can quickly grill them on a chargrill pan.

Heat an outdoor grill or chargrill pan. Wipe the steaks dry and brush with a little oil on each side. Sprinkle with freshly ground black pepper. Grill the steaks for 2 minutes each side over direct high heat. Remove and let rest for 5 minutes, then slice the steak.

Eat the tacos with a little of the spicy mayo, a spoonful of meat and lots of the kimchee-style slaw.

NOTES

Kalbi steaks are thinly sliced beef ribs cut across the bones rather than in between. Their texture is similar to skirt steak.

If you don't have gochugaru, you can substitute 2 teaspoons red chilli flakes.

Go to any Chinatown and you'll find hooks of this glossy red meat in the windows. Sliced over rice, stuffed in buns or added to fried rice, it's a cherished Chinese dish. Char sui gets its colour from fermented red bean curd and its shine from maltose sugar and is then roasted or steamed. I've taken liberties with the hard-to-find ingredients to create a much more accessible grilled version.

GRILLED STICKY CHAR SUI PORK

SERVES 4

PREP 10 MINUTES, PLUS 4 HOURS MARINATING

COOK 25 MINUTES

3 pork tenderloins (fillets)
3 tbsp honey
3 garlic cloves, crushed
1 tablespoon grated ginger
150 ml (5 fl oz) hoisin sauce
3 tbsp oyster sauce
1 tbsp dark soy sauce
1 tbsp sriracha or other hot chilli sauce
2 tsp five-spice powder

steamed or XO fried rice (see page 192), Ginger pickles (see page 53) and steamed greens, to serve

Place the pork in a zip lock bag. In a bowl, mix all of the remaining ingredients together, keeping back 2 tablespoons of the honey. Pour over the meat and zip the bag shut. Leave in the refrigerator overnight to marinate if possible or for at least 4 hours.

Preheat a chargrill pan or an outdoor grill and use indirect heat so the meat is not sitting directly over the flames. An easy way to do this with charcoal is to arrange a drip tray in the middle of the grill and arrange the hot coals around it.

Remove the meat from the marinade, scraping the leftovers into a bowl. Place the pork on the grill and brush with the marinade. After 5 minutes, turn over and glaze the other side. Continue to repeat this until the meat is sticky and a little charred on the edges, about 20 minutes. Near the last 10 minutes of cooking, drizzle the honey over each side to give it an extra dose of stickiness. Cover with foil and let sit for 5 minutes until slicing.

Serve with steamed or XO fried rice, pickles and steamed greens.

If you're buying a great steak, it doesn't need much embellishment, which is why a simple teriyaki glaze is perfect (see photo on page 142). It's a classic Japanese grill glaze that always draws applause for meat, fish or tofu. Serve it with a Sliced tomato salad (see page 87) and boiled new potatoes for a minimal-fuss dinner.

TERIYAKI T-BONE STEAKS

SERVES 4
PREP 10 MINUTES, PLUS
2 HOURS MARINATING
COOK 10 MINUTES

2 T-bone steaks, sirloin,
   porterhouse or fillet
1 garlic clove
1 tbsp sesame oil
1 tbsp togarashi spice mix

TERIYAKI GLAZE
75 ml (2½ fl oz) Japanese soy sauce
75 ml (2½ fl oz) mirin
75 ml (2½ fl oz) sake
2 tbsp caster sugar
juice of 3 lemons

lemon quarters and Sliced tomato
   salad (see page 87), to serve

To make the teriyaki glaze, add all the ingredients to a small saucepan and mix together.

Place the steaks in a zip lock bag. Pour 3 tablespoons of the teriyaki glaze over the meat. Zip the bag shut and refrigerate for 2 hours or overnight.

Bring the remaining teriyaki glaze to a boil and simmer over a low heat until it becomes slightly thicker and syrupy, about 5 minutes. Let cool.

Heat an outdoor grill or chargrill pan. Remove the steaks from their marinade and discard any liquid. Smash the garlic to a paste with a little sea salt. Dry the steaks with paper towels, brush with oil, the smashed garlic and crack plenty of black pepper over.

Add the steaks to the grill over direct high heat. Let cook for a few minutes and then turn the steaks over. Start to brush with the teriyaki glaze on both sides. Sprinkle the togarashi over. It should take about 2–3 minutes for each side of the steaks.

Remove from the grill and let the steaks rest for 5 minutes in foil. Serve the steaks with lemon quarters and a tomato salad.

Thai pastes and chilli jams are an easy cheat for throwing together a quick dinner. Yellow curry paste has a tremendous tangy lemongrass flavour and puts the oomph into these fish parcels. Tom yum paste, nam prik or red curry paste can also be used. I like the Mae Ploy brand. Steam up some fresh green vegetables and rice to make this a more substantial meal.

COCONUT FISH PARCELS
WITH MANGO SALSA

SERVES 4
PREP 10 MINUTES
COOK 20 MINUTES

4 thick chunky fish fillets
   (200 g/7 oz each)
4 tsp yellow or red curry paste
4 tsp fish sauce
100 ml (3½ fl oz) coconut cream
4 tbsp toasted coconut

ROASTED CHILLI SAUCE
150 g (5½ oz) caster sugar
150 ml (5 fl oz) rice vinegar
2 tsp red chilli flakes
juice 1 lime
1 tbsp fish sauce

MANGO SALSA
2 small ripe but firm mangoes, diced
3 small shallots, sliced
small handful chopped
   coriander (cilantro)

lime wedges and coriander
   (cilantro), to serve

8 sheets foil or 4 large (25 cm/
   10 inch) squares of banana
   leaf, for wrapping

To make the roasted chilli sauce, heat the sugar and rice vinegar in a small saucepan. After it boils, let it reduce for 5 minutes and then remove from the heat. Add the chilli flakes, lime juice and fish sauce. Let cool and pour into a serving bowl.

To make the mango salsa, mix all the ingredients in a small bowl and set aside.

If using banana leaves, turn on your stovetop hob and run each banana leaf through the heat. This will soften them and make them pliable for wrapping. For the foil, use two for each parcel.

Place the fish on top of the banana leaf or foil squares. Mix the curry paste, fish sauce and coconut cream together. Spread over all sides of the fish. Sprinkle with the toasted coconut.

If using foil, bring the top and bottom together and fold twice for a secure package. Bring the sides in and fold the edges twice too. Make sure there is a little room so that the fish can steam. If using banana leaf, then fold the bottom over the fish and bring the top down. Bring the sides all the way over and secure with a toothpick. The fish can be wrapped and then refrigerated for up to 8 hours before grilling.

Preheat an outdoor grill. Grill over medium direct heat for about 12 minutes and then remove.

Serve the fish with lime wedges and scattered with coriander, along with the roasted chilli sauce for dipping and the mango salsa. Add rice and steamed greens for a more substantial meal.

NOTES
Halibut, barramundi and salmon all work well in this dish.

If you have lime leaves, place a few under the fish to add another zip of citrus. I like to keep a stash of leaves in the freezer for when I need them.

HOT POTS & CURRIES

I stumbled on this gorgeous roast chicken in a buzzy food market in Kuala Lumpur where it whirled around on a rotisserie until shiny and lacquered like an old antique. The stallholder served it on top of fragrant rice with a drizzle of soy chilli sauce and cucumbers. I decided to have a stab at recreating it at home. Baby chickens work best as the meat doesn't dry out.

SLOW-ROAST COCONUT and LEMONGRASS CHICKEN

SERVES 4
PREP 10 MINUTES, PLUS
2 HOURS MARINATING
COOK 1 HOUR 15 MINUTES

6 lemongrass stems, save the ends
8 lime leaves, 3 finely chopped
2 garlic cloves
3 tbsp fish sauce
3 tbsp palm or soft brown sugar
2 tbsp chopped coriander (cilantro)
4 poussin (baby chickens)
75 ml (2½ fl oz) coconut cream
zest 2 limes

SWEET-AND-HOT SAUCE
3 tbsp sambal oelek chilli sauce
2 small shallots, sliced
2 tbsp sweet soy sauce
   (kecap manis)
juice 2 zested limes

steamed rice, to serve

Finely chop the inner part of the lemongrass. In a food processor or blender, make the marinade by blending the chopped lemongrass, chopped lime leaves, garlic, fish sauce, 1 tablespoon of the sugar and the coriander until it forms a fine paste.

Place the birds in a shallow baking dish or a large zip lock bag. Pour the marinade in and rub all over. Ideally leave overnight in the refrigerator, but if you only have a few hours, that's okay too.

Preheat the oven to 190°C (375°F) or 170°C (325°F) fan forced. Drain the chickens and place in a roasting dish lined with foil, a cast iron frying pan or roasting dish. Stuff the leftover pieces from the lemongrass and the remaining whole lime leaves into the cavity of the birds.

Mix the coconut cream and remaining sugar with the lime zest. Microwave or heat for 1 minute to melt the sugar. Brush some over the chickens and bake for 10 minutes, and then brush more on. Keep repeating until the coconut cream has gone shiny.

Check the meat after it has roasted for 1 hour 15 minutes. When you pierce the skin near a leg, the juices should run clear. If not, give them another 15 minutes.

To make the sweet-and-hot sauce, mix all the ingredients together and set aside.

Serve the baby chickens with steamed rice and the sweet-and-hot sauce to pass around.

NOTE
If you don't have sambal oelek, you can substitute another chilli sauce or 1 finely chopped large fresh red chilli.

Curry was introduced to Japan by the British navy in the 1800s and it's now one of the country's most loved dishes. Poured over crispy katsu or udon (see page 70) or eaten as a stew, the fruity sauce is a favourite. Most Japanese households use S & B instant roux cubes, which look like chocolate squares. They work beautifully, but aren't easy to get hold of here. This is my homemade version.

JAPANESE VEGETABLE MISO CURRY

SERVES 4
PREP 15 MINUTES
COOK 30 MINUTES

3 tbsp vegetable oil
2 onions, sliced in half moons
2 tsp grated ginger
2 garlic cloves, grated
1 apple, peeled, cored, grated
1 tbsp tomato paste
    (concentrated purée)
3 tbsp pale (shiro) miso
3 tbsp mild curry powder
2 tbsp Japanese soy sauce
2 tbsp Worcestershire sauce
750 ml (26 fl oz) stock
3 large carrots
1 red capsicum (pepper)
2 large sweet potatoes

steamed rice, chopped spring onion
    (scallion) and black sesame seeds,
    to serve

In a large saucepan, heat the oil. Add the onion, ginger, garlic and apple. Season well and sauté for 8 minutes or until soft.

Add the tomato paste and stir for 1 minute. Add the miso, curry powder, soy, Worcestershire and the stock. Bring to a simmer.

Cut the carrots, capsicum and sweet potatoes into chunks and then add to the curry. Cook until the vegetables are soft, but still al dente.

Serve with steamed rice and chopped spring onion with sesame seeds sprinkled over.

NOTES

For the stock you can use good-quality bought chicken or vegetable stock or make the Dashi stock on page 77.

This homemade sauce can also be used for chicken, meat or fish. Simply omit the sweet potatoes and add 500 g (1 lb 2 oz) of protein.

Malaysia has a whirling variety of influences on its cooking – Chinese, Indian, Thai, Portuguese and Indonesian just for starters. The Chinese-influenced recipes are known as Nonya cuisine and this is one such hallmark dish. The homemade curry paste doesn't take long to make, but you could save time by using red curry paste. Serve up some warm roti alongside to dip into the coconut-spiced sauce.

CAPTAIN'S CURRY (AYAM KAPITAN)

SERVES 4
PREP 15 MINUTES
COOK 1 HOUR 15 MINUTES

4 chicken legs and 4 thighs on the bone, with skin
1 tbsp vegetable oil
400 ml (14 fl oz) coconut milk
3 tbsp toasted coconut flakes
100 g (3½ oz) tamarind purée
2 tsp five-spice powder
2 star anise
2 cinnamon sticks
juice 2 limes
6 lime leaves

SPICE PASTE
4 lemongrass stems
75 g (2½ oz) small shallots
4 garlic cloves
1 thumb-sized red chilli, seeded
6 long dried red chillies, seeded
20 g (¾ oz) galangal, sliced
20 g (¾ oz) ginger, sliced
3 macadamia nuts
1 tsp ground turmeric
2 tbsp fish sauce or 2 tsp shrimp paste (belacan or kapi)

steamed rice, roti, chopped coriander (cilantro) and toasted coconut flakes (optional), to serve

To make the spice paste, finely chop the inner part of the lemongrass and add to the blender with all the other spice paste ingredients and 50 ml (2 fl oz) water. Blend to a very fine paste.

Season the chicken well. Heat a large saucepan and add the vegetable oil. Sear the chicken pieces until browned all over, about 3 minutes each side. Remove from the pan, pour off excess oil and add the spice paste. Cook over medium heat for 5–6 minutes until cooked through.

Return the chicken pieces to the pan and stir in the coconut milk, toasted coconut flakes, tamarind and dried spices.

Simmer over a low heat with the lid placed partially over the pan for 1 hour–1 hour 15 minutes or until the chicken is tender and nearly falling off the bone. During the last 5 minutes of cooking, add the lime juice and the lime leaves.

Serve the curry with steamed rice, roti, chopped coriander and, optionally, the toasted coconut.

NOTES

If using a prepared red curry paste, then use 75 g (2½ oz). The homemade paste in this recipe makes 200 g (7 oz), but it is less concentrated than ready-made.

To toast the coconut, bake in an oven preheated to 170°C (325°F) or 150°C (300°F) fan forced for 8 minutes until golden at the edges.

Burma is bordered by Thailand, India, Laos and China and the country's food is freckled with spices, citrus and fishy influences from all of them. I love the simplicity of this fish curry. It's delicate but still delivers a punch of quintessential Burmese flavours – hot, sour, salty and slightly bitter.

BURMESE FISH AND TOMATO CURRY

SERVES 4
PREP 10 MINUTES
COOK 20 MINUTES

750 g (1 lb 10 oz) firm fish fillets
1 tsp ground turmeric
3 tbsp fish sauce
1 tbsp vegetable oil
4 ripe tomatoes, seeded, diced
1 tsp paprika
300 ml (10½ fl oz) fish or
   vegetable stock
juice 2 limes

CHILLI PASTE
2 small shallots, sliced
2 garlic cloves, sliced
3 cm (1¼ inch) ginger, sliced
2 thumb-sized chillies, sliced

steamed rice, coriander (cilantro),
   lime quarters and crispy fried
   shallots, to serve

Slice the fish fillets into chunky pieces about 6 cm (2½ inches). Place in a bowl with the turmeric and fish sauce. Leave to marinate while you make the chilli paste.

To make the chilli paste, in a mortar and pestle or food processor, grind the shallots, garlic, ginger and chillies with a little sea salt until they are puréed.

In a medium saucepan, heat the oil. Add the chilli paste and sauté for 8 minutes until soft and slightly golden. Add the tomatoes, paprika and the stock. Let the liquid simmer for 10 minutes and then add the fish and lime juice. Cook until the fish is bright white, about 2–3 minutes.

Serve the curry with steamed rice, fresh coriander, lime quarters and some crispy fried shallots.

NOTE
Halibut, tilapia, barramundi, salmon and even prawns all work well in this dish.

Vinegar lovers need to stop here for the Philippine's best-known dish. Seared chicken is poached in a vinegar, ginger and garlic bath until it falls off the bone. After trying many different vinegars, for me cider comes out the winner for the best depth and flavour. Here rice vinegar is too mild and white wine results in an acidic sauce. Pork ribs or belly are also delicious, but give them longer to simmer.

ADOBO CHICKEN

SERVES 4
PREP 10 MINUTES
COOK 45 MINUTES

3 tbsp sesame oil
6 chicken legs or 12 drumsticks
    and thighs on the bone
8 cm (3½ inch) ginger, julienned
10 garlic cloves
3 onions, cut in small wedges
125 ml (4 fl oz) light soy sauce
250 ml (9 fl oz) cider vinegar
2 tbsp caster sugar
1 tsp red chilli flakes

steamed rice, coriander (cilantro)
    leaves and sliced spring onions
    (scallions), to serve

In a heavy saucepan, heat the sesame oil. Add the chicken legs and brown on both sides, about 5 minutes. Remove from the pan and add the ginger and whole garlic cloves and sauté over medium heat until golden, about 5 minutes.

Add the onion, soy, vinegar, sugar and chilli flakes to the pan. Cover with a lid and cook over low heat for 20 minutes. Remove the lid and cook for another 15 minutes. The sauce will thicken and become more concentrated as it cooks.

Serve the chicken with steamed rice and a sprinkling of coriander and sliced spring onions.

Mapo dofu means 'pockmarked old lady', and references the curdled texture of the tofu used in this Sichuan dish. The secret to the spicy pork sauce is the chilli bean paste called toban jiang, which is made from fermented broad beans, garlic and chilli. The Japanese do their own version (mabo don) featuring a similar combination. This makes a quick weekday meal spooned up over rice.

MAPO DOFU

SERVES 4
PREP 10 MINUTES
COOK 20 MINUTES

200 g (10½ oz) silken tofu
1 tbsp sesame oil
500 g (1 lb 2 oz) minced
　　pork or beef
4 spring onions (scallions)
2 garlic cloves, finely chopped
1 tbsp grated ginger
1 tbsp Sichuan peppercorns

CHILLI SAUCE
1½ tbsp cornflour
3 tbsp light soy sauce
4 tbsp Shaoxing rice wine
250 ml (9 fl oz) stock
3 tbsp toban jiang
　　(hot chilli bean paste)
2 tbsp roasted chilli flakes
　　in oil, drained, plus extra

steamed rice, to serve

Drain the tofu and place in thick paper towels to remove the excess water. Slice into 3 cm (1¼ inch) cubes and set aside.

In a large wok, heat half the oil. Brown the meat until crisp on the edges, about 5 minutes. Drain any excess oil. Scrape the meat out of the pan and add the remaining oil. Chop the white spring onions and pan-fry with the garlic and ginger until golden, about 2 minutes. Add the meat back in and stir together.

To make the chilli sauce, mix the cornflour with 2 tablespoons water, then mix all the sauce ingredients together and set aside.

In a small frying pan, toast the Sichuan peppercorns for 30 seconds and then grind in a mortar and pestle or spice grinder.

Pour the sauce over the meat and let simmer for 10 minutes. Just before eating, add the tofu pieces and let simmer for another 2 minutes. Sprinkle with the chopped green spring onions and Sichuan peppercorns.

Serve the mapo dofu over steamed rice with an extra dollop of roasted chilli flakes.

NOTE
You can order the toban jiang online or find it in the Asian section of many supermarkets. If you can't get hold of it, try using the same amount of miso mixed with 1 tablepoon chilli paste instead.

This Hunan specialty, which was one of Mao's favourite dishes, is a bit like pork candy. The meat is braised in a sugary rice wine and soy liquid and slowly softens until it is meltingly tender and coated in a sticky sweet-and-sour sauce. Chinese rock sugar makes this dish very authentic and you can easily buy it online, but feel free to use normal caster sugar instead.

CHAIRMAN MAO'S PORK BELLY

SERVES 4
PREP 20 MINUTES
COOK 1 HOUR 20 MINUTES

900 g (2 lb) rindless pork belly
2 tsp five-spice powder
1 tbsp sesame oil
3 cm (1¼ inch) ginger, julienned
6 spring onions (scallions)
60 g (2¼ oz) rock sugar or
    4 tbsp caster sugar
60 ml (2 fl oz) dark soy sauce
30 ml (1 fl oz) light soy sauce
90 ml (3 fl oz) Shaoxing rice wine
2 tbsp black or rice vinegar
1 star anise
2 whole dried chillies

steamed rice, to serve

Bring a large pot of water to the boil. Add the pork and boil for 10 minutes. Drain and rinse under cold water. Chop the meat into 3 cm (1¼ inch) pieces and toss with the five-spice.

Heat the oil in a heavy-based frying pan over a medium–high heat. Add the pork in batches and brown on both sides. Remove from the pan and add the ginger and the chopped white part of the spring onions. Sauté for 3–4 minutes until soft and then add the finely crushed rock sugar. Stir constantly until melted.

Add the pork back in and stir for 1–2 minutes. Add the soy sauces, rice wine, vinegar, star anise, dried chilli and 500 ml (17 fl oz) water. Place a lid on top and turn the heat down to the lowest setting. Let cook for 30 minutes and then remove the lid. Continue cooking for 30 minutes more, stirring periodically, or until the meat is tender and sticky.

Remove the spices and discard. Serve the pork sprinkled with the chopped green spring onions and bowls of rice alongside.

Sukiyaki was the first dish I ate in Tokyo, in an old-school restaurant dedicated to this glorious hot pot. My legs kept falling asleep, crouched under the low table, but I was mesmerised by the cast iron pot with the vegetables and beef bubbling away in a sweet soy and dashi liquid. It's all served piping hot at the table with little bowls of beaten egg to dip vegetables or meat in (that's optional for you).

 SUKIYAKI

SERVES 4
PREP 20 MINUTES
COOK 15 MINUTES

2 tsp vegetable or sesame oil
500 g (1 lb 2 oz) beef sirloin,
    semi-frozen, very thinly sliced
200 g (7 oz) shiitake mushrooms
½ small napa cabbage, cut in chunks
2 carrots, sliced
2 onions, sliced in thick half moons
150 g (5½ oz) ready-cooked
    shirataki noodles or glass noodles
    (mung bean noodles) (optional)

SUKIYAKI BASE
125 ml (4 fl oz) Japanese soy sauce
125 ml (4 fl oz) mirin
3 tbsp sake
2 tbsp caster sugar
400 ml (14 fl oz) Dashi stock (see
    page 77) or vegetable stock

steamed rice, togarashi spice mix
    and chopped spring onions
    (scallions), to serve

Place the oil in a heavy medium–large saucepan. When the oil is hot, add the beef and brown gently for about 2–3 minutes.

To make the sukiyaki base, in a small bowl mix together the soy, mirin, sake, sugar and dashi stock until the sugar is dissolved. Pour this over the meat.

Score a cross in the top of the shiitake mushrooms. Add along with the other ingredients in composed sections to the pan and simmer for 5 minutes. The vegetables should still have a nice al dente bite to them.

Serve the sukiyaki with bowls of rice and togarashi and spring onion to sprinkle over.

NOTES
If you have access to an Asian store you can often buy the meat already thinly sliced. It's typically sold frozen, so you can stock up for future dinners.

Shirataki noodles are yam-based noodles, which are gluten and rice free and have practically no calories. They are usually sold in packs, already cooked. They have a chewy texture and hold this even when heated through. You can use glass noodles instead, which are soaked in hot water first, or just leave the noodles out.

I can't implore you enough to make your own dashi stock for this recipe as it makes all the difference. It can be made in 15 minutes with just two ingredients.

DONABE MAGIC

CLAY POT COOKING FOR SIMMERING STEWS, SOUPS, STEAMING OR RICE

BUY

Japanese iga-yaki donabe (the best quality available) or other cooking pot, made from durable clay.

WHY USE A DONABE?

Fast way to cook healthy food.
Clay enhances food's flavour.
Can be taken to the dinner table for sharing.
Retains a high heat.

CREATE YOUR OWN

DASHI BASE OR STOCK

POTENTIAL FLAVOURS

SOY SAUCE
GINGER
MISO
MIRIN
SAKE
GARLIC
RICE VINEGAR
CURRY POWDER
CHILLI

PICK YOUR PROTEIN

THIN SLICES OF BEEF,
DUCK, CHICKEN OR PORK
TOFU
SHELLFISH
FIRM FISH
MEATBALLS
GYOZA
EGGS

CHOOSE YOUR VEGGIES + NOODLES

VEG

CABBAGE (ALL TYPES)
CARROTS
SWEET POTATOES
SPRING ONIONS
TURNIPS
ENOKI, OYSTER OR SHIITAKE MUSHROOMS
SPINACH
LOTUS ROOT OR DAIKON
SQUASH OR PUMPKIN
ONIONS
BROCCOLI
BOK CHOY
KALE OR GREENS
MIZUNA

NOODLES (OPTIONAL)

UDON
RAMEN
SOBA
SHIRATAKI

SERVE WITH...

RICE
YUZO KOSHO/YUZU JUICE
SOY OR PONZU
MISO DIPPING SAUCE
HOT YELLOW MUSTARD (KARASHI)
WASABI
TOGARASHI SPICE MIX
CHILLI PASTE OR CHILLI OIL

Donabe should translate to 'warm and fuzzy blanket' because it soothes your soul. The name actually refers to the earthenware pot that's used to make steaming hot pots, rice and stews. Crafted from a highly durable clay that can sit over a flame without cracking, it is prized for maintaining an even temperature while cooking and staying hot at the table and is perfect for social gatherings.

CHICKEN MEATBALL AND MISO DONABE

SERVES 4
PREP 20 MINUTES
COOK 20 MINUTES

1 tbsp sesame oil
2 garlic cloves, crushed
3 tbsp miso
1 tsp hot chilli sauce
2 tbsp Japanese light soy sauce
60 ml (2 fl oz) mirin
700 ml (24 fl oz) stock
4 carrots, cut into slim batons
4 bok choy or other greens, halved
150 g (5½ oz) small shiitake
    mushrooms

MEATBALLS
500 g (1 lb 2 oz) boneless
    skinless chicken thighs
1 tbsp Japanese soy sauce
2 spring onions (scallions),
    finely chopped
1 tbsp cornflour
1 tbsp grated ginger

steamed rice, yuzu juice or yuzu
    kosho, chopped green spring
    onions (scallions) and togarashi
    spice mix, to serve

To make the meatballs, start by puréeing the chicken in a food processor to the texture of mince. Remove and place in a medium bowl. Add the soy, spring onion, cornflour and ginger, then give it a good grinding of black pepper. Roll into small meatballs, about 3 cm (1¼ inches) wide. You can now pan-fry the meatballs using 2–3 teaspoons vegetable oil until browned on all sides or just poach them in the hot broth.

Pour the sesame oil into a donabe or heavy, large saucepan with a fitted lid. Sauté the garlic over medium–low heat and then add the miso, chilli sauce, soy and mirin. Cook for 1 minute or until the miso melts into the liquid. Pour in the stock and bring to a boil. Add the meatballs and carrots, cover and turn the heat down to a low simmer. Cook for 8 minutes and then add the bok choy. Let simmer for 2 minutes, add the mushrooms and then bring the pot to the table. The bok choy should have an al dente texture.

Serve in shallow bowls with a bowl of rice for everyone and a small bowl of yuzu juice or yuzu kosho, chopped green spring onions and togarashi spice mix, to sprinkle over.

NOTES
Any meat or even prawns can be used to make the meatballs, so substitute any you wish.

For the stock you can use good-quality bought chicken stock or make the Dashi stock on page 77.

Brushed on barbecued meat, seafood or used as the base for curries and hot pots, caramel is Vietnam's signature flavour. It sounds unorthodox, but once mixed with fish sauce and lime it transforms into a magic elixir for Vietnamese cooking. Traditionally this dish is cooked in small clay pots, but you can use a donabe or heavy saucepan with a lid.

VIETNAMESE CARAMELISED FISH HOT POT

SERVES 4
PREP 10 MINUTES
COOK 15 MINUTES

1 thumb-sized red chilli, seeded
2 garlic cloves
4 cm (1½ inch) ginger
1 tbsp vegetable oil
2 tbsp palm or soft brown sugar
2 tbsp fish sauce
1 tbsp tamarind purée
200 ml (7 fl oz) stock
600 g (1 lb 5 oz) salmon fillets

chopped coriander (cilantro) or mint
   leaves, steamed rice, green
   vegetables like bok choy and
   lime wedges, to serve

Place the chilli, garlic and ginger in a food processor and pulse until chopped. Alternatively, you can hand chop them.

In a medium pan, donabe or large clay hot pot, heat the oil. Add the chopped mixture and cook over medium heat until softened, about 5 minutes. Pour in the sugar mixed with 1 tablespoon water. Heat for about 2–3 minutes until melted and bubbling. Add the fish sauce, tamarind and stock. Bring this to a simmer.

When you are ready to eat, add the salmon fillets to the liquid. Place a lid on and let simmer for 5–8 minutes or until the fish is done (thicker fish might take another minute or two).

Add some fresh coriander or mint to the hot pot and serve with steamed rice, green vegetables and lime wedges.

It's up for debate as to whether this is a soup or a curry. The Thais consider it the former, but for me it's a main meal. Khao soi gai is from Chiang Mai, in the north of Thailand, and what makes it superior to other curries is the addition of curry powder and the fried crispy noodles that adorn it. The extra trimmings of pickled shallots, chillies and heaps of fresh herbs don't hurt either.

CHIANG MAI CURRIED NOODLES ⟨KHAO SOI GAI⟩

SERVES 4
PREP 20 MINUTES
COOK 30 MINUTES

1 tbsp vegetable oil
75 g (2½ oz) red curry paste
2 tsp mild curry powder
50 ml (2 fl oz) tamarind purée
1 tbsp palm or soft brown sugar
400 ml (14 fl oz) coconut milk
100 ml (3½ fl oz) chicken stock
2 tbsp fish sauce
1 tbsp soy sauce
juice 2 limes
700 g (1 lb 9 oz) boneless
   skinless chicken thighs
300 g (10½ oz) egg noodles
vegetable oil, for frying

Pickled red chilli and shallots
   (see page 52) and chilli sauce
   (nam prik, sriracha or sambal
   oelek) (optional), julienned spring
   onion (scallion), coriander
   (cilantro) or mint leaves and lime
   wedges, to serve

In a medium saucepan, heat the vegetable oil. Add the curry paste and cook for 5 minutes. Add the curry powder, tamarind and sugar. When the sugar is melted, add the coconut milk, stock, fish sauce, soy and lime juice. Bring to a gentle boil and then add the chicken. Simmer for 20 minutes or until the meat is tender.

Set aside 100 g (3½ oz) of the noodles and divide into four piles. Heat the oil in a wok or deep medium saucepan until it reaches 180–190°C (350–375°F) or when a small piece of bread instantly sizzles. Add one portion of the dry noodles. They will fry instantly so quickly remove them and drain on paper towels. Continue until you have fried all four portions.

Boil the other 200 g (7 oz) of noodles for about 4 minutes or until al dente. Drain and divide into four large bowls. Ladle the curry over and top and serve with the pickled red chillies and shallots, chilli sauce, the spring onion, fresh herbs, lime wedges and fried noodles.

NOTE
You can use a prepared red curry paste for this (Mae Ploy is good) or try my homemade Master red curry paste (see page 78) if you have more time.

Most of us are familiar with red curry paste, but the yellow paste from southern Thailand is pretty special too. Made with lemongrass, chillies and spices, it has a sour tanginess. The Mae Ploy brand is my go-to and I don't think you can improve on their pastes. I've used duck breasts here, but you could try legs. If doing so, sear them first and let them slowly poach in the curry liquid for 1 hour until tender.

SOUR YELLOW CURRY DUCK WITH PINEAPPLE AND LIME LEAVES

SERVES 4
PREP 10 MINUTES
COOK 45 MINUTES

4 duck breasts
75 g (2½ oz) yellow curry paste
1 tbsp palm or soft brown sugar
2 tbsp fish sauce
50 ml (2 fl oz) tamarind purée
400 ml (14 fl oz) coconut milk
juice 2 limes
2 lemongrass stems
6 lime leaves (optional)
75 g (2½ oz) pineapple

steamed rice, green beans, handful
  each Thai basil and coriander
  (cilantro) and lime wedges,
  to serve

Preheat the oven to 200°C (400°F) or 180°C (350°F) fan forced.

Heat a medium saucepan. Place the duck breasts, fat side down, into the pan. Turn the heat down to the lowest setting and let the fat render until it is very thin, about 10 minutes. Remove the duck breasts and place them in a roasting tin.

Drain off the majority of the oil from the pan and add the curry paste. Sauté over medium heat for 5 minutes. Add the sugar and cook until melted, about 1 minute. Add the fish sauce, tamarind and coconut milk. Add the lime juice and give the lemongrass stems a bash with the back of a knife and then add to the curry. Simmer for 15 minutes to bring the flavours together.

About 20 minutes before serving, roast the duck breasts, uncovered, for 8 minutes. Remove and cover with foil to rest. Add the lime leaves (if using) and pineapple cut into 3 cm (1¼ inch) pieces to the curry and let simmer for a few minutes.

Serve up four bowls of rice and the green beans. Slice the duck and place on top of the rice. Pour the curry sauce over each serving, top with fresh herbs and serve with the lime wedges.

This very homely Thai dish is low on effort, but extremely tasty. A clay pot isn't necessary, but once you get hooked on using one it's hard to stop, and it lends a certain earthiness to the food as it bubbles away. Chinatown markets and Asian shops sell them cheaply or you can use a Japanese donabe (see page 177).

CLAY POT NOODLES *with* PORK *and* PRAWNS «GOONG OB WOONSEN»

SERVES 4
PREP 10 MINUTES
COOK 20 MINUTES

200 g (7 oz) glass noodles
   (mung bean noodles)
8 large raw peeled prawns
1 tbsp sesame oil
2 onions, sliced in half moons
5 cm (2 inch) ginger, julienned
8 slices pork belly
100 g (3½ oz) Chinese celery with
   leaves or regular celery, chopped

PEPPERCORN PASTE
3 garlic cloves
1 tsp black peppercorns
5 coriander (cilantro) roots or
   1 tbsp chopped stems

OYSTER SOY SAUCE
3 tbsp oyster sauce
1 tbsp dark soy sauce
2 tbsp fish sauce
100 ml (3½ fl oz) stock

coriander (cilantro) leaves and
   chopped green spring onions
   (scallions), to serve

Soak the glass noodles in warm water for 10 minutes and then drain.

Use a sharp knife to slice down the back of each prawn and rinse out the vein.

To make the peppercorn paste, in a mortar and pestle pound the garlic, pepper and coriander root together.

In a large clay hot pot or heavy large saucepan with a fitted lid, heat the oil. Sauté the peppercorn paste, onion and ginger over medium heat for 5–7 minutes until soft. Chop the pork into 5 cm (2 inch) pieces and toss with the flavourings in the pot. Arrange the pork in the bottom in a single layer. Top with the noodles and celery. Lay the prawns on top of this and pour the oyster soy sauce ingredients over.

Place the lid on and cook over medium heat for 10–12 minutes. You can also bake in a preheated 200°C (400°F) or 180°C (350°F) fan forced oven for the same amount of time.

Serve immediately with fresh coriander and green spring onion sprinkled over.

NOTES

Traditionally Chinese celery is used, which is a very thin variety of regular celery. You can use bog standard celery, but pick the finer sticks at the top along with the leaves.

Either use one large clay hot pot or two small ones. Alternatively, you can use a large donabe clay pot or a medium cast iron or heavy lidded pot.

Cha ca fish is so popular in Hanoi they have an entire street dedicated to it! The restaurants have only one thing on the menu – turmeric and ginger marinated fish with dill and rice noodles. It's wok-fried at your table, on a charcoal brazier, and served with lime chilli sauce and roasted peanuts.

VIETNAMESE PRAWNS (CHA CA) WITH DILL AND RICE NOODLES

SERVES 4
PREP 10 MINUTES, PLUS
10 MINUTES MARINATING
COOK 10 MINUTES

2 garlic cloves, chopped
2.5 cm (1 inch) ginger, chopped
2 tsp ground turmeric
2 tbsp fish sauce
2 tbsp vegetable oil
400 g (14 oz) large raw peeled
  and butterflied prawns with tails
200 g (7 oz) rice vermicelli
6 spring onions (scallions), chopped
large handful dill stalks and
  leaves, chopped

CHILLI LIME SAUCE
100 ml (3½ fl oz) lime juice
60 ml (2 fl oz) fish sauce
3 tbsp palm or soft brown sugar
1 thumb-sized red chilli, thinly
  sliced, or 2 Thai chillies, sliced

chopped roasted peanuts, lime
  wedges and coriander (cilantro),
  to serve

To make the marinade, in a medium bowl mix together the garlic, ginger, turmeric, fish sauce and 1 teaspoon of the oil.

Use a sharp knife to slice down the back of each prawn and rinse out the vein. Add the prawns to the marinade and marinate for about 10 minutes.

To make the chilli lime sauce, in a small bowl mix together all the ingredients and stir to dissolve the sugar. If you like more heat, you can add more chillies, but I've kept it fairly mild.

In a large bowl, pour boiling water over the noodles. Leave to sit while you cook the prawns.

Heat a large sauté pan with the remaining oil over medium–high heat. Add the spring onions and dill and cook for 1 minute and then add the prawns. Stir-fry until they are cooked through, 2–3 minutes.

Drain the noodles and spoon over the stir-fried prawns.

Serve with a bowl of the chilli lime sauce, chopped roasted peanuts, lime wedges and fresh coriander.

NOTE

Catfish is the local fish used for cha ca in Vietnam, but it's not so common outside of the country. A sturdy thick fish is required in this dish to withstand the heat without breaking up. Monkfish, barramundi or halibut have the density, but I have found fat, large prawns work best. They soak up all the flavours without sticking to the wok.

A recent invention, XO is a crazy-good sauce of dried seafood, chilli, garlic, soy and ham. The Hong Kong chef who created it christened it 'XO', which means 'extra old', borrowing the name from a luxury cognac. There are more complicated ways of producing it, but this is a pared-down version. Traditionally XO includes dried scallops, but they're impossible to get hold of unless you visit Chinatown.

XO FRIED RICE

SERVES 4 AND MAKES 150 G
(5½ OZ) CHEAT'S XO SAUCE
PREP 10 MINUTES
COOK 40 MINUTES

200 g (7 oz) sugar snap peas
175 g (6 oz) baby corn, sliced
2 tbsp vegetable oil
2 eggs, lightly beaten
1 onion, chopped
3 cm (1¼ inch) ginger, chopped
400 g (14 oz) jasmine or basmati
    rice, cooked al dente, or 6 cups
    cooked rice, cooled
2 tbsp oyster sauce
1 tbsp dark soy sauce

CHEAT'S XO SAUCE
2 tbsp dried shrimp
100 g (3½ oz) prosciutto, chopped
4 finger-length red chillies, chopped
2 tbsp finely chopped ginger
6 garlic cloves
3 large shallots, chopped
1 tbsp palm or soft brown sugar
1 tbsp soy sauce
90 ml (3 fl oz) peanut (groundnut) oil

sriracha or other hot chilli sauce,
    to serve

The night before cooking, place the dried shrimp in a bowl, cover with water and soak overnight.

Place the drained dried shrimp in a food processor and blend until fine. Add in all of the other XO ingredients, except the oil, and blend again until you have a paste.

Heat a frying pan and add the peanut oil. Pour in the XO sauce and cook over a low heat for 30 minutes until it turns a deep-brown colour and has a sticky consistency. Remove from the heat and let cool.

Bring a saucepan of water to a boil. Add the sugar snaps and baby corn and blanch for 1 minute. Drain and rinse under cold water. Dry on a tea towel.

Heat a large wok. Add 1 tablespoon of the vegetable oil. Pour the eggs in a roll around the pan so you get a thin layer. Roughly chop up with a spatula and then place in a bowl. Pour the remaining oil into the pan and add the onion and ginger. Sauté over medium heat until softened, about 3 minutes.

Add 75 g (2½ oz) of the XO sauce (refrigerate the rest), the cold rice, baby corn, sugar snap peas and the oyster and soy sauces. Keep stir-frying for 5 minutes until everything is warmed through.

Serve the fried rice with a red chilli sauce like sriracha. This dish also works nicely alongside the Grilled sticky char sui pork (see page 156).

NOTE

Once you've made a batch of XO, use it to stir-fry rice and seafood, as a paste for steamed fish or to toss through noodles. If you're not up for making your own, then buy a prepared jar.

'Bulgogi', or 'fire meat', is a carnivore's dream. The waft of Korean BBQ is everywhere in Seoul – meat is marinated in garlic, sesame oil and soy and dramatically sizzled on a smoking grill in the centre of your table. Little plates of banchan (pickles or salads) are served alongside. As most of us don't have a table grill, a wok is the next best thing. Feel free to substitute beef or pork for chicken.

CHICKEN BULGOGI STIR-FRY

SERVES 4
PREP 20 MINUTES, PLUS
1 HOUR MARINATING
COOK 10 MINUTES

500 g (1 lb 2 oz) boneless skinless
  chicken thighs, cut into slices
1 tbsp sesame oil
1 large onion, sliced in half moons
1 tbsp sesame seeds, toasted

BULGOGI MARINADE
60 ml (2 fl oz) soy sauce
3 tbsp caster sugar
½ small onion, quartered
60 ml (2 fl oz) mirin
6 cm (2½ inch) ginger, peeled
6 garlic cloves, peeled
2 tbsp chopped pineapple
2 tbsp gochugaru
  (Korean chilli flakes) or
  2 tsp red chilli flakes
1 tbsp sesame oil

steamed rice, chopped spring onion
  (scallion) and kimchee, to serve

To make the bulgogi marinade, add all the ingredients to a food processor and blend until fine.

Place the chicken in a zip lock bag or glass bowl. Pour the marinade over and refrigerate for up to 1 hour, covered. Bring back to room temperature before cooking.

Heat ½ tablespoon of the sesame oil in a large wok or big frying pan until very hot. Add the onion and stir-fry for a few minutes. Add the chicken and marinade and keep stirring constantly until it's cooked through, about 5 minutes. Add the sesame seeds and stir again. The chicken should have a sticky, glossy sauce.

Serve the chicken with steamed rice and finely chopped spring onion, with kimchee on the side.

NOTE

One of the secrets of a good bulgogi marinade is a little fruit, which acts as an acid to tenderise the meat. Nashi pear is very typically used, but I like the sweetness of pineapple.

Sichuan peppercorns are a mystical ingredient. Their lemon-like taste, with a slightly numbing effect on the tongue, is a powerhouse. But, more importantly, they act as a taste enhancer, magnifying other flavours. Alongside star anise and cinnamon, they are one of the key ingredients in five-spice powder. You can substitute boneless chicken thighs or vegetables in this mouth-watering stir-fry.

FAT SICHUAN PRAWNS STIR-FRY WITH CRISPY CHILLI SAUCE

SERVES 4
PREP 15 MINUTES
COOK 15 MINUTES

1 tbsp Sichuan peppercorns
50 g (2 oz) cornflour
1 tbsp sea salt
400 g (14 oz) large raw
   peeled prawns
200 g (7 oz) fine green beans
60 ml (2 fl oz) vegetable oil
2 thumb-sized red chillies, sliced
2 garlic cloves, thinly sliced
4 spring onion (scallions), cut into
   5 cm (2 inch) lengths

CRISPY CHILLI SAUCE
2 tsp cornflour
2 tbsp roasted chilli flakes
   in oil, drained
2 tbsp black vinegar
2 tbsp light soy sauce
1 tbsp hoisin sauce

steamed rice, to serve

In a small frying pan, heat the Sichuan peppercorns until fragrant, about 30 seconds. Roughly grind in a spice mill or mortar and pestle and then mix in a shallow bowl with the cornflour, sea salt and a good grinding of black pepper.

Use a sharp knife to slice down the back of each prawn and rinse out the vein. Toss the prawns in the spicy flour and coat well. Shake off excess.

To make the crispy chilli sauce, first dissolve the cornflour in 1 tablespoon water, then in a small bowl combine with all the other ingredients.

Blanch the beans in boiling water for 1 minute, then rinse under cold water and drain.

Add the vegetable oil to the wok and fry the chilli and garlic until golden, about 1 minute. Remove from the pan. Add the prawns and fry until pink and slightly curled.

Drain off almost all the oil and add the beans to the wok along with the spring onion. Stir-fry for 1 minute and then add the sauce. Keep stir-frying until warm and sticky, about 1–2 minutes.

Remove the stir-fry from the heat and serve with steamed rice. Sprinkle with the fried garlic and chillies.

Sambal is a pounded chilli paste that can also include garlic, ginger, tamarind, fish sauce and lemongrass. It has many variations, but Malay sambal oelek is one of the most versatile and easily sourced. It's the lazy person's dream for cooking as you can dollop it into stir-fries, dressings and dipping sauces. Mixed with tamarind and sweet soy, it creates a perfect hot, salty and sour sauce for any stir-fry.

SPICY TAMARIND PRAWNS
《SAMBAL UDANG》

SERVES 4
PREP 15 MINUTES
COOK 10 MINUTES

3 tbsp tamarind purée
1 tbsp fish sauce
1 tbsp sweet soy sauce
   (kecap manis)
1 tbsp palm or soft brown sugar
400 g (14 oz) large raw prawns
1 tbsp vegetable oil
1 onion, sliced in half moons
10 small ripe cherry tomatoes

SAMBAL PASTE
2 tbsp sambal oelek chilli sauce
1 large shallot
2 garlic cloves

steamed rice, julienned spring
   onions (scallions) and steamed
   vegetables, to serve

In a small bowl, mix the tamarind, fish sauce, soy sauce, sugar and 2 tablespoons water together until the sugar has dissolved, then set aside.

Use a sharp knife to slice down the back of each prawn and rinse out the vein.

To make the sambal paste, place the ingredients in a food processor or blender and purée until fine.

In a wok, heat the vegetable oil and cook the paste until darkened, about 5 minutes. Add the onion and stir-fry for about 2–3 minutes. Add the prawns and stir-fry until slightly pink, about 1 minute, and then add the tamarind sauce and tomatoes. Keep stir-frying until the sauce is thickened and sticky.

Serve the prawns with steamed rice, spring onions and a bowl of steamed vegetables.

NOTE
If you don't have sambal oelek, you can substitute another chilli sauce or 2 finely chopped fresh red chillies.

Whole fried fish is a foodie highlight when travelling in Thailand. It's served propped up with skewers and you pluck off the flesh and dip it in a tamarind or lime chilli dressing. For home cooking, this extravaganza isn't so practical, but you can achieve the same deliciousness using fillets. A green papaya or carrot salad served alongside keeps textures lively and contrasts nicely with the hot, crisp fish.

CRISPY RED SNAPPER WITH GREEN PAPAYA SALAD

SERVES 4
PREP 15 MINUTES
COOK 15 MINUTES

50 g (2 oz) basmati rice
4 tbsp cornflour
1 tsp red chilli flakes
4 thick firm white fish fillets
   (150 g/5½ oz each)
vegetable oil, for frying

CITRUS DRESSING
1 garlic clove
1 cm (½ inch) ginger
2 tbsp palm or soft brown sugar
45 ml (1½ fl oz) fish sauce
100 ml (3½ fl oz) lime juice
60 ml (2 fl oz) orange juice

GREEN PAPAYA SALAD
300 g (10½ oz) green papaya or
   cabbage, shredded
1 large carrot, julienned
4 Thai shallots, thinly sliced
2 lime leaves, shredded (optional)
1 small handful each coriander
   (cilantro), Thai basil and mint
   leaves, plus extra
4 tbsp crispy fried shallots
2–3 small Thai red chillies, sliced

In a dry frying pan over low heat, slowly brown the rice for about 10 minutes until it is light brown. Place in a mortar and pestle or blender and finely grind. Pour into a shallow tray. Remove 2 tablespoons and mix in a bowl with the cornflour and chilli flakes and season with sea salt and black pepper.

To make the citrus dressing, in a mortar and pestle pound the garlic and ginger. Add the sugar, fish sauce and citrus juices until the sugar is dissolved. Taste for additional sugar or fish sauce – it should be sour, salty and somewhat sweet. Set aside for serving.

Place the green papaya salad ingredients in a bowl and set aside.

Using a sharp knife, score a diamond pattern into the skin side of the fillets. Toss each one in the chilli flour and shake off any excess.

Heat the oil in a wok or deep medium saucepan until it reaches 180–190°C (350–375°F) or when a small piece of bread instantly sizzles. Fry the fillets for about 2–3 minutes until golden and crisp.

Pour two-thirds of the dressing over the salad and toss well. Arrange on plates and top with the fish. Pour the remaining dressing over the top and sprinkle with the ground rice and extra herbs.

NOTE
Red snapper and sea bass work well in this dish.

Garlic, chilli, shallots, tamarind and shrimp paste are just some of the umami ingredients in Thai chilli paste/jam (nam prik pao), an essential taste in Thai soups, sauces and stir-fries. Find jars of it online or visit your local Asian shop. Mixed with a little soy and fish sauce, it makes a swift but magical stir-fry sauce.

THAI CHICKEN STIR-FRY *WITH* CASHEWS *AND* CHILLI JAM SAUCE

SERVES 4
PREP 10 MINUTES
COOK 10 MINUTES

100 g (3½ oz) baby corn
1 tbsp vegetable oil
500 g (1 lb 2 oz) boneless skinless
   chicken thighs
4 garlic cloves, finely chopped
2 red chillies, thickly sliced
2 red capsicums (peppers)
1 onion, sliced in half moons
50 g (2 oz) roasted cashews

CHILLI JAM SAUCE
2 tbsp Thai chilli paste/
   jam (nam prik)
1 tbsp fish sauce
2 tbsp light soy sauce
juice 1 lime
4 tbsp oyster sauce

Thai basil or regular and steamed
   rice, to serve

To make the chilli jam sauce, in a small bowl mix together all the ingredients and set aside.

Bring a pot of water to a boil. Blanch the baby corn for 2 minutes, then drain, rinse under cold water and drain again.

Heat a large wok until very hot and add half the oil. Cut the chicken into 3 cm (1¼ inch) pieces. In batches, brown the chicken pieces. I like to leave them for 2–3 minutes on one side initially so they take on a nice golden colour. Stir-fry until golden on all sides, another minute or so, then transfer to a bowl.

Heat the remaining oil in the wok. Add the garlic and chilli and keep the heat on medium so they don't burn. Stir-fry for 1 minute or so until golden. Cut the capsicums into thick pieces and then add with the onion, cashews and baby corn. Heat for 1 minute, then pour in the chilli jam sauce and add the chicken. Stir-fry until everything is heated through and the chilli jam sauce is thick.

Serve the stir-fry with steamed rice and basil sprinkled over.

WOK WISDOM

BUY

CARBON STEEL WOK
FLAT-BOTTOMED IS BEST
AS BIG AS POSSIBLE
LIGHT, INEXPENSIVE ASIAN BRAND

USE iT FOR

FRYING
STIR-FRYING
SMOKING MEAT OR FISH

SEASON

Heat until screaming hot!

Once it turns purple and blue, remove from heat and let it cool.

Rub oil all over the surface (use lots of paper towels). Heat again until smoking, then cool down.

A well-seasoned wok makes wok hey (AKA – 'the breath of the wok') as it infuses your food with smoky aromas.

TECHNiQUE

1

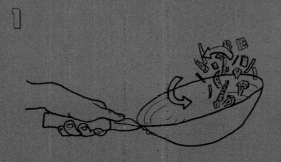

2 ✛

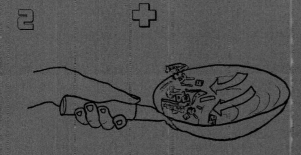

Jerk the wok back and forth on the heat,
or use two long spoons to stir quickly!

DO

Heat the wok first,
then swirl the oil in.

Prep all ingredients on
a tray before cooking.

Cook your meat, fish or tofu
first, remove, and then
stir-fry vegetables.

Add the sauce last.

DON'T

Add too much oil at once –
gradually add as needed.

Fry ginger and garlic over
high heat – keep heat low
otherwise they will burn.

Put too much food in – cook
two batches if necessary.

Malaysia, Indonesia and Singapore all share a love of mee goreng, though recipes range from using rice noodles to thick yellow wheat ones. Any seafood, vegetables or meat can be used, but the concept of the sauce is similar – sweet soy, tamarind and chilli – clinging to the noodles for a gorgeous, sticky stir-fry.

SWEET SOY CHICKEN NOODLES (MEE GORENG)

SERVES 4
PREP 10 MINUTES
COOK 20 MINUTES

300 g (10½ oz) dried thick egg
  noodles (the very yellow ones)
2 tbsp vegetable oil
500 g (1 lb 2 oz) chicken thighs,
  cut into bite-size pieces
3 garlic cloves, chopped
1 small onion, sliced in half moons
300 g (10½ oz) bok choy or other
  greens, chopped
6 spring onions (scallions), chopped
2 large handfuls beansprouts

SWEET SOY SAUCE
4 tbsp sambal oelek chilli sauce
  or sriracha
2 tbsp tamarind purée
75 ml (2½ fl oz) sweet soy sauce
  (kecap manis)
45 ml (1½ fl oz) light soy sauce

Bring a large pot of water to a boil. Add the noodles and boil until very al dente. Drain and leave in the sieve.

To make the sweet soy sauce, in a small bowl mix together the chilli paste, tamarind, sweet soy sauce and the regular soy sauce.

In a large wok, heat the oil. Add the chicken pieces and sauté until browned and cooked through, about 8–10 minutes. Remove from the wok and set aside.

Add the garlic and onion to the wok and sauté for 2–3 minutes. Add the boy choy, noodles, chicken, spring onion and the sweet soy sauce. Keep stirring over a very high heat until the noodles are sticky and warmed through.

Toss the beansprouts through the noodles and serve.

Nasi goreng is an addictive rice stir-fry that's topped with a fried egg. I couldn't stop eating it in Malaysia and found it easy to replicate at home. Traditional recipes can include a complicated base involving shrimp paste, fried anchovies and an ingredient list as long as your arm, but sometimes less is more. This recipe is less fish-fragrant and I've thrown in chopped pineapple for a fresh flavour.

FRIED RICE WITH CRISPY FRIED EGG (NASI GORENG)

SERVES 4
PREP 15 MINUTES
COOK 10 MINUTES

400 g (14 oz) basmati rice
1 tbsp tamarind purée
4 tbsp sweet soy sauce
    (kecap manis)
1 tbsp fish sauce
2 garlic cloves
2 shallots
handful coriander (cilantro),
    stalks and leaves
3 cm (1¼ inch) ginger
2 tbsp vegetable oil
1 red thumb-sized chilli, thinly sliced
100 g (3½ oz) green beans, chopped
50 g (2 oz) pineapple, chopped
4 eggs

crispy fried shallots, cucumber
    slices and lime wedges, to serve

Boil the rice until al dente, about 8 minutes, then drain.

In a small bowl, mix together the tamarind purée, kecap manis and fish sauce.

Place the garlic, shallots, the coriander stalks and ginger in a food processor and pulse until chopped.

Heat 1 tablespoon oil in a wok and fry the chopped garlic mixture and the chilli for 2–3 minutes. Add the beans and pineapple, fry for 2 minutes, then add the rice. Pour in the tamarind mixture and toss together so that it coats the rice. Remove from the heat.

Heat the remaining tablespoon of oil in a large frying pan until very hot. Crack in the eggs and fry over a high heat for 1 minute until the whites are crispy at the edges, but the yolks soft.

Spoon the rice into four bowls, then top each with a fried egg, a sprinkling of the crispy fried shallots and coriander leaves. Serve with slices of cucumber and lime wedges.

Pad krapow gai translates as 'fried holy basil chicken' and is the ultimate Thai street food dish. Minced chicken is stir-fried with fish sauce, garlic and chillies, and is topped off with a fried egg. Thai basil does give it an authentic flavour, but you can substitute the regular variety if you like.

THAI STIR-FRIED CHICKEN
WITH BASIL ⟨PAD KRAPOW GAI⟩

SERVES 4
PREP 15 MINUTES
COOK 10 MINUTES

500 g (1 lb 2 oz) boneless skinless
    chicken thighs
3 tbsp fish sauce
50 ml (2 fl oz) chicken stock
1 tbsp Thai sweet soy sauce (or use
    kecap manis or dark soy)
2 tbsp vegetable oil
6 garlic cloves, crushed slightly
2 thumb-sized red chillies, sliced
1 onion, diced
100 g (3½ oz) fine green beans
3 handfuls Thai basil leaves
4 eggs

steamed rice, lime wedges and
    Pickled red chillies (see page 52),
    to serve

Place the trimmed chicken thighs in a food processor and pulse until roughly minced.

Combine the fish sauce, chicken stock and sweet soy sauce in a small bowl.

Heat the wok, add half the oil and sear the chicken until golden, about 5 minutes. Push the chicken to one side of the wok. Add the garlic and chilli and sauté over low heat until the garlic is golden, about 2–3 minutes.

Add the onion and the halved green beans and stir-fry for another 2–3 minutes.

Add the sauce and basil and stir-fry for a further 2 minutes. Remove from the heat.

Heat the remaining oil in a frying pan. Crack the eggs in and fry until crisp at the edges, about 2–3 minutes.

Serve the chicken with the fried eggs on top, steamed rice, lime wedges and pickled chilli.

You can use very simple vegetables for this classic Japanese stir-fry, such as cabbage, onion and carrots, or add some bacon, chicken or prawns. The real stars of this noodle dish are the thick chewy noodles and zingy sauce. Soy, mirin and tonkatsu sauce are the key ingredients for yaki udon or yaki soba. Tonkatsu is sold under a popular brand name of Bull-Dog sauce and tastes like English HP sauce.

YAKI UDON STIR-FRY

SERVES 4
PREP 10 MINUTES
COOK 10 MINUTES

1 tbsp sesame oil
1 onion, sliced in half moons
2 garlic cloves, chopped
75 g (2½ oz) kale, green cabbage
  or greens, chopped
2 carrots, cut in thin coins
8 shiitake mushrooms, halved
250 g (9 oz) dried udon or
  450 g (1 lb) frozen or fresh
  (see page 70)
1 tbsp black or white sesame seeds,
  toasted

YAKI UDON SAUCE
3 tbsp Japanese light soy sauce
3 tbsp tonkatsu or HP sauce
2 tbsp mirin
1 tbsp rice vinegar

To make the yaki udon sauce, in a small bowl mix together all the sauce ingredients.

In a large wok or big frying pan, heat the oil until very hot. Add the onion, garlic, kale and carrot. Stir-fry until slightly softened, about 3–4 minutes.

Add the yaki udon sauce, shiitakes and noodles and stir-fry until the sauce is sticky and the noodles are warmed through.

Sprinkle the noodles with the sesame seeds to serve.

NOTE

To make your own tonkatsu sauce, mix together 1 tablespoon each of Worcestershire sauce, caster sugar and tomato ketchup.

A plastic tub of gochujang is a must-have for your ingredient arsenal. It's a powerhouse chilli paste made from red chilli flakes, rice flour, malt syrup and fermented soya beans. Possessing the salty depth of miso, it has a sweeter taste and is very spicy. Use it to make the sauce for bibimbap, BBQ glazes or pour into a quick stir-fry sauce.

SPICY KOREAN STIR-FRY VEGETABLES

SERVES 4
PREP 10 MINUTES
COOK 10 MINUTES

2 tbsp vegetable oil
2 onions, sliced in half moons
1 garlic clove, chopped
1 tbsp finely chopped ginger
2 zucchini (courgettes)
2 carrots
125 g (4½ oz) cabbage
100 g (3½ oz) kale or other greens
4 spring onions (scallions), chopped
1 tbsp black and white sesame seeds

GOCHUJANG SAUCE
1 tbsp gochujang
   (Korean chilli paste)
2 tbsp rice vinegar
2 tbsp light soy sauce
2 tbsp mirin or rice wine
1 tbsp honey

steamed rice, to serve

To make the gochujang sauce, mix the ingredients together in a small bowl and whisk until smooth.

In a large wok, heat 1 tablespoon of the oil. Stir-fry the onion, garlic and ginger until softened, about 2 minutes. Slice the zucchini into batons, julienne the carrots and thickly slice the cabbage.

Add another tablespoon of the oil to the pan and then add the zucchini, carrot and cabbage. Keep stir-frying until the vegetables are slightly softened. Pour in the sauce and add the kale, cut into chunks, and stir-fry for 2 more minutes. It should be hot and the sauce sticky on the vegetables.

Sprinkle the vegetables with the spring onion and sesame seeds. Serve with rice.

NOTES

Any vegetables, noodles, rice or protein will slot in here. Try sliced sweet potato, green beans, broccoli, firm tofu, meat or seafood.

If you can't get gochujang sauce, then substitute equal portions of miso and chilli sauce.

This northern Chinese noodle dish is served with a meat sauce that's not shy on the chilli oil, garlic or Sichuan peppercorns. Traditionally lamb is used, but hand chopping the shoulder meat can be laborious, so I've used minced pork. Feel free to use any fat noodles like udon (see page 70) or even pappardelle, which mimic hand-cut noodles. I've also included a recipe (see page 214) to make your own.

SPICY XIAN PORK NOODLES

SERVES 4
PREP 10 MINUTES
COOK 20 MINUTES

400 g (14 oz) fresh fat or wide
  noodles or 250 g (9 oz) dried
1 red chilli, thinly sliced
1 tbsp sesame seeds, toasted

SICHUAN SAUCE
2 tsp cumin seeds
2 tsp coriander seeds
2 tsp Sichuan peppercorns
2 tsp cornflour
4 tbsp roasted chilli flakes
  in oil, drained, plus 2 tbsp oil
3 cm (1¼ inch) ginger, chopped
5 spring onions (scallions)
3 garlic cloves, chopped
400 g (14 oz) minced pork
4 tbsp light soy sauce
5 tbsp black vinegar
2 tbsp Shaoxing rice wine

To make the Sichuan sauce, in a small frying pan toast the spices until fragrant, about 30 seconds. Remove and roughly grind in a mortar and pestle or spice grinder. Set aside.

Dissolve the cornflour in 1 tablespoon water.

Heat a large wok. Add the roasted chilli oil and sauté the ginger, chopped white spring onion parts and the garlic over medium heat until cooked, about 3 minutes. Add the pork and brown for about 4 minutes until crisp, breaking up the pieces. Add the soy, chilli flakes sediment, black vinegar, rice wine, cornflour water and toasted spices. Keep stir-frying until sticky and the sauce is thick. Remove from the heat.

Boil a large pot of water. If using the fresh noodles, boil for 2–3 minutes – they are done when they start to float to the top of the water. Drain and set aside. If using dried, boil for 6–7 minutes and then drain. Give them an extra rinse of hot water to remove any extra starch.

Add the noodles to the sauce and stir-fry over medium heat using two long spoons. When everything is hot and sticky, pour into four large bowls and top with the chopped green parts of the spring onion, sliced red chilli and toasted sesame seeds.

NOTE
Warning – not all roasted chilli flakes in oil are created equal! Most Asian shops sell various brands of chilli oil or crispy chillies in oil, typically with the flakes, garlic and black beans (basically all the sludge) beneath the oil. My favourite brand is Lao Gan Ma, packaged in a red jar with a photo of a Chinese lady on the front (the name translates to 'old lady'). It has a cult status around the world and once you've tried it, you might find yourself stockpiling extra jars in your cupboard.

There are many varieties of homemade thick Chinese noodles (la mian). Lanzhou, from the Northwest, are hand-pulled and stretched just before boiling, but are difficult to do at home. Biang biang mian from Shaanxi, named for the snapping sound of the dough as it hits the worktop to stretch into noodles, are also popular. My dough is simply rolled out and cut, which is no different to making pasta.

HAND-CUT NOODLES ⟨LA MIAN⟩

MAKES 450 G (1 LB) NOODLES
PREP 1 HOUR, PLUS 1 HOUR SITTING
COOK 5 MINUTES

250 g (9 oz) plain flour
125 g (4½ oz) 00 flour
   or pastry flour
½ tsp salt, plus extra
150 ml (5 fl oz) warm water
cornflour, for sprinkling

Add the flours and salt to a standing electric mixer with a dough hook or a large mixing bowl. Start the motor or mixing by hand and then slowly pour in the water. Mix well until it comes together into a ball. If it's too sticky, then add a tiny bit of flour. Likewise if it doesn't come together into a ball, add 1 teaspoon of water at a time until it does. Bread flours can differ, so adjust accordingly.

Knead the dough in the mixer or else on the worktop for 10–12 minutes. When the dough is smooth and silky, cover with plastic wrap and let sit for 1 hour.

Line two big trays with non-stick baking paper and sprinkle with cornflour. Roll the dough out into a large rectangle on a floured surface about 2 mm (1/16 inch) thick. Slice into strips, about 3 cm (1¼ inches) wide. Roll up eight to ten strands into a nest and sprinkle with cornflour.

You can cook the noodles straight away or, if using later, then leave to sit out for 1 hour. This will firm them up so they don't get sticky. If you want to use them the next day or later in the evening, then line a tray with baking paper dusted with flour, arrange the nests of noodles with more flour and then top with more baking paper. Wrap everything in plastic wrap and refrigerate if the cooking time is going to be more than 4 hours after making. The noodles can also be frozen.

To cook, bring a very large pot of water to the boil. Add a couple of tablespoons of salt to the water and then add the noodles. When the noodles float to the top, they are ready. Drain and use in stir-fries or soups.

NOTE

These thick, chewy noodles are the perfect base instead of rice for any stir-fry. Try with the Fat Sichuan prawns stir-fry (see page 195) or the Stir-fried broccoli (see page 215). They're also delicious added to thick, meaty soups like the Tawainese beef noodle soup (see page 58).

If you're putting together an Asian feast and want to round out some of the other meat dishes, then this simple green vegetable stir-fry is ideal. You can use any greens you like, such as savoy cabbage, kale, greens, bok choy or green beans. It sounds strange to blanch the broccoli first, but it produces a better result.

STiR-FRiED BROCCOLi WITH GARLiC AND OYSTER SAUCE

SERVES 4
PREP 10 MINUTES
COOK 5 MINUTES

300 g (10½ oz) Chinese broccoli
   (gai larn) or tenderstem broccoli
2 tbsp oyster sauce
2 tbsp Shaoxing rice wine
1 tbsp light soy sauce
3 tsp sesame oil
3 garlic cloves, thinly sliced
1 thumb-sized red chilli, thinly sliced
100 g (3½ oz) sugar snap peas

Blanch the broccoli for 1 minute, drain and rinse in cold water. Dry on a tea towel.

Mix the oyster sauce, rice wine and soy together in a small bowl and set aside.

When you are close to serving, heat the sesame oil in a large wok. Over medium heat, stir-fry the garlic and chilli for 1 minute or until golden.

Turn up the heat and throw in the sugar snaps and the broccoli and stir-fry for 1 minute to heat through. Pour the sauce over and stir-fry for 1 more minute until everything is hot and sticky.

Nothing beats an icy granita when the weather is hot. It's the perfect showcase for sweet seasonal fruit. The traditional method of scraping every hour can be tiresome, so this is a shortcut for the same result. Just freeze it solid and then bash it up.

NO-SCRAPE FRUITY GRANITA

SERVES 4
PREP 10 MINUTES
FREEZE 4 HOURS

150 g (5½ oz) caster sugar
500 g (1 lb 2 oz) fruit (remove peel
    and big seeds before weighing)
1 tbsp lime, lemon or yuzu juice

Fruit suggestions: blackberry,
    passion fruit pulp, mango, green
    melon, lychee, raspberry,
    strawberry, kiwi, watermelon,
    pineapple, papaya

In a saucepan, heat 250 ml (9 fl oz) water and the sugar and boil for 5 minutes until the sugar is melted and slightly syrupy.

Pour into a container and chill until room temperature. It will take about 10 minutes in the freezer.

In a blender, combine the peeled fruit with the citrus and sugar syrup. Purée until smooth. Pour it into a large zip lock bag or alternatively pour it into a shallow tray. You may want to double bag it to make sure there are no leaks. Let it freeze completely. Try and lay the bag flat in the freezer so that it doesn't form a large block. The thinner the layer of frozen fruit is, the easier to bash up.

When ready to serve, bash the bag with a rolling pin. You may need to pop a little hole in the bag to let out some air. Alternatively, you can chop the frozen granita into 5 cm (2 inch) pieces and blend in a food processor until it has a gravel-like texture. You will need to do it in two batches.

You can serve the granita straightaway or else freeze again in a covered container. If freezing, then press the surface with non-stick baking paper so it doesn't become freezer burnt.

NOTE

If you have a Vitamix or Nutribullet it will finely purée this granita, but a food processor may leave little seeds or fibre you may prefer to sieve (only strawberries, raspberries, pineapple or blackberries would require this).

Japanese matcha powder is a wonder to mix into frostings, ice cream or cream for its Shrek-like colour and astringent taste. Here it pairs beautifully with chocolate for a showstopper dessert. I've cooked many chocolate cakes in my lifetime, but this one is the ultimate. My sister-in-law Amy divulged her family recipe to me and the cake has a springy moist texture and a pure cocoa flavour, but is not too rich.

DEVIL'S FOOD CAKE WITH MATCHA FROSTING

SERVES 8

PREP 45 MINUTES, PLUS 1 HOUR CHILLING

COOK 40 MINUTES

250 ml (9 fl oz) boiling water
75 g (2½ oz) cocoa powder
350 g (12 oz) plain flour
350 g (12 oz) caster sugar
2 tsp baking powder
1 tsp bicarbonate of soda
    (baking soda)
1 tsp salt
2 eggs
250 ml (9 fl oz) milk
125 ml (4 fl oz) vegetable oil
2 tsp vanilla extract

MATCHA FROSTING
325 g (11½ oz) salted butter,
    at room temperature
650 g (1 lb 7 oz) icing
    (confectioners') sugar
2 tsp vanilla extract
2 tbsp matcha powder
3 tbsp milk

Preheat the oven to 180°C (350°F) or 160°C (315°F) fan forced. Grease and line two 20 cm (8 inch) or three 18 cm (7 inch) round springform cake tins.

Pour the boiling water into a measuring jug and add the cocoa. Whisk the mixture smooth and let cool while you measure out all the remaining ingredients.

Pour the remaining dry ingredients into the bowl of a standing electric mixer or use a large bowl and electric hand mixer.

In another bowl, whisk the eggs, milk, oil and vanilla extract. When the cocoa mixture has cooled enough, whisk into the egg and milk mixture.

On a slow speed, add the liquid until combined. Beat for 1 minute on slow speed. Pour the mixture into the tins. It will seem very liquid, but will bake up very light. Bake for 35–40 minutes on the centre rack of the oven. Cool in the tins and then remove.

To make the matcha frosting, in the bowl of the standing mixer, whisk the butter on slow speed for 6–7 minutes until pale and fluffy. It's imperative that your butter is at room temperature to get a smooth, silky texture. Add the sifted icing sugar, 2 tablespoons at a time, keeping the speed slow. When finished, add the vanilla, sifted matcha and milk and keep beating until the mixture is very smooth. If it's too thick, add another tablespoon of milk.

Place one cake on a serving platter. Spread a thick layer of frosting to sandwich the two or three cakes. Ice the sides first and then the top. If you want to get a perfect finish, try 'crumbing' the cake by first spreading a thin layer of frosting around the outside and top of the cake until everything is smoothed at the same level. Place in the fridge for 1 hour and the cake will set. Remove and then ice the cake with more frosting.

If you want a light dessert after a rich or meaty menu, this is the ticket. The vanilla bean and ginger-infused syrup elevates any fruit and it's particularly good over ice cream. Make a colourful platter with these tropical varieties or choose your own favourites.

TROPICAL FRUIT SALAD with GINGER and VANILLA SYRUP

SERVES 4–6
PREP 15 MINUTES
COOK 5 MINUTES

150 g (5½ oz) caster sugar
1 vanilla bean, split
4 slices ginger
2 ripe mangoes
2 ripe papaya
½ small pineapple
2 kiwi, thickly sliced
55 g (2 oz) large toasted
    coconut flakes

Place the sugar, vanilla bean, ginger and 150 ml (5 fl oz) water in a saucepan and bring to the boil. Cook for about 4 minutes or until the sugar is dissolved and the mixture is syrupy. Remove and allow to cool. Scrape the vanilla bean seeds into the syrup and remove the ginger.

Cut the mango, papaya and pineapple into 4 cm (1½ inch) batons or chunks. Arrange all the fruit on a small platter, pour over the syrup and garnish with the toasted coconut.

NOTE
To toast the coconut, bake in an oven preheated to 170°C (325°F) or 150°C (300°F) fan forced for 8 minutes until golden at the edges.

Most Asian food is fairly light and healthy, so you can feel virtuous treating yourself to a wicked creamy chocolate pie with crushed peanut brittle. This is also very good with toasted coconut or bananas sliced up on top.

CHOCOLATE CUSTARD PIE WITH PEANUT BRITTLE CRUMBLE

SERVES 8
PREP 30 MINUTES, PLUS
3½ HOURS SETTING
COOK 5 MINUTES

275 g (9½ oz) crunchy biscuits, such as Hobnobs
100 g (3½ oz) butter, melted
250 g (9 oz) caster sugar
50 g (2 oz) cocoa powder
40 g (1½ oz) cornflour
650 ml (22½ fl oz) evaporated milk
4 tbsp butter
1 tsp vanilla extract

PEANUT BRITTLE CRUMBLE
100 g (3½ oz) caster sugar
50 g (2 oz) roasted salted peanuts

TOPPING
300 ml (10½ fl oz) thick (double) cream
3 tbsp caster sugar
1 tsp vanilla extract

Preheat the oven to 200°C (400°F) or 180°C (350°F) fan forced. Place the biscuits in a food processor with the melted butter. Pulse until completely combined. Press into a deep 25 cm (10 inch) pie pan. Bake for 5 minutes or until crisp. Remove and let cool.

Pour the sugar, cocoa, cornflour and a pinch of sea salt into a saucepan. Whisk in the milk and keep stirring until blended. Cook over medium heat, stirring constantly, until it comes to a boil. Let it boil for 1 minute and then remove from the heat.

Whisk in the remaining butter and vanilla extract. Pour over the crust and press a sheet of plastic wrap over the surface to prevent a hard layer forming. Let cool for 30 minutes and then refrigerate for 2–3 hours until set.

To make the peanut brittle crumble, in a non-stick frying pan melt the sugar over low–medium heat without stirring. Have the peanuts ready on a piece of non-stick baking paper. When the sugar is melted and starts to turn a light caramel colour, pour over the nuts. Let sit for 10 minutes and then break into pieces. Chop it roughly with a knife.

To make the topping, whip the ingredients together until soft peaks form. Spread over the set pie. Sprinkle the peanut brittle crumble over the pie when close to serving.

This is going to sound complicated, but I urge you to give it a go. You will need a sugar thermometer and standing mixer, but if you follow the directions you won't fail. Homemade marshmallows are sooo much better than bought ones and a nice treat to serve after an Asian extravaganza. This makes a large number of pieces, but if you halve the recipe the one egg white is hard to beat to stiff peaks.

COCONUT MARSHMALLOWS

MAKES 30 MARSHMALLOWS
**PREP 40 MINUTES, PLUS
2 HOURS SETTING**
COOK 12 MINUTES

200 g (7 oz) desiccated
   (grated dried) coconut or
   large flakes, chopped
10 sheets gelatine (20 g/¾ oz)
500 g (1 lb 2 oz) caster sugar
4 tsp liquid glucose
2 large egg whites
1 tbsp vanilla extract

Preheat the oven to 170°C (325°F) or 150°C (300°F) fan forced. Spread the coconut out over two baking trays. Bake for about 10–12 minutes or until the edges turn golden, stirring once to evenly cook. Remove and let cool.

Line a 30 x 20 cm (12 x 8 inch) brownie tin or something similar in size (it's ideal if the tin has straight square corners) with baking paper. Let the paper hang over the sides so you can lift out the marshmallows later. Pour half of the coconut into the tin.

Soak the gelatine sheets in a bowl of cold water and leave to sit until softened while you make everything else.

In a large, deep saucepan (be sure it's deep enough to hang a sugar thermometer on the side) add the sugar, glucose and 200 ml (7 fl oz) water. Keep the heat on medium until the sugar has dissolved. Now turn up the heat and boil until it reaches the firm ball stage on the sugar thermometer, about 125°C (250°F). If you don't own a thermometer, then pour a little of the syrup into a cup of very cold water and if it sets to a firm but flexible ball, then it's done.

While the sugar is cooking, beat the egg whites until stiff. A standing electric mixer is best for this but you can use an electric hand mixer with a large bowl. After the syrup has reached the right temperature, pour it quickly into a jug and start slowly drizzling it into the stiff egg whites as they whisk. Don't worry about the hard dribbles on the side as they will get incorporated as it continues to increase in volume. Once all the syrup is in, squeeze the gelatine sheets from the water and add, one at a time, until completely incorporated. Pour in the vanilla and whisk for another 10 minutes.

Scrape the mixture into the tin lined with toasted coconut. Spread evenly and then top with the remaining coconut. Leave to sit for 2 hours or until set.

Lift the marshmallow out of the tin using the paper as handles. Set on a chopping board and cut into 6 cm (2½ inch) square pieces. Use a paper towel to wipe your knife in between cutting so it's not too sticky. Roll the squares in the excess toasted coconut (from the tin) and coat all sides. Store the marshmallows in a tin lined with baking paper and covered for up to 1 week.

A playful Asian take on an Australian classic, these sandwiched biscuits are sometimes called melting moments. They are made with custard powder instead of the standard cornflour, which adds a creamy vanilla flavour, though either ingredient works fine (custard powder is annatto-flavoured cornflour). The buttercream can be flavoured with citrus or berries, so feel free to swap flavours.

PASSION FRUIT YO YO BISCUITS

MAKES 30 SANDWICHED BISCUITS
PREP 20 MINUTES
COOK 15 MINUTES

DOUGH
250 g (9 oz) salted butter,
    at room temperature
220 g (8 oz) plain flour
100 g (3½ oz) icing
    (confectioners') sugar
75 g (2½ oz) custard powder
    or cornflour
flesh of 1 passion fruit (about 1 tbsp)

FILLING
125 g (4½ oz) butter,
    at room temperature
150 g (5½ oz) icing
    (confectioners') sugar
2 passion fruit, flesh sieved

Preheat the oven to 180°C (350°F) or 160°C (315°F) fan forced.

To make the dough, in a standing electric mixer or using a large bowl with an electric hand mixer, beat the butter until pale and creamy, about 2–3 minutes. Add the flour, icing sugar, custard powder or cornflour and the passion fruit flesh with seeds. Beat for another 2–3 minutes until smooth.

Line two baking trays with baking paper. Roll 2 heaped teaspoons of the dough into small balls. You will make about 60 balls and they will seem small, but they get bigger when baked. Place on the trays and press with a fork dusted in cornflour to flatten them, being sure to space them out on the trays with 4 cm (1½ inches) between each biscuit. Bake for 12–15 minutes or until light and set. Remove and cool completely.

To make the filling, place the butter in the bowl of the electric mixer and beat for a minute or two until creamy. Add the sugar and beat until smooth, about 2 minutes. Add the passion fruit pulp and seeds and beat again until smooth.

Sandwich the biscuits together using the passion fruit filling. Store in a covered container until ready to serve. These will keep for up to a week.

Salted caramel is a winning duo, so why not instead pop miso into caramel for the salty kick? This caramel sauce doesn't require any thermometers and all the ingredients get thrown in the pan together. Bananas work well, but you can also use other fruits like peaches, plums or apples. If miso isn't your thing, just pop a few star anise and a teaspoon of five-spice in to infuse with an Asian pop.

BANANA WAFFLES WITH MISO CARAMEL SAUCE

SERVES 4
PREP 10 MINUTES
COOK 15 MINUTES

500 ml (17 fl oz) vanilla ice cream
4 waffles
6 small ripe but still firm bananas
3 tbsp chopped roasted cashews
3 tbsp toasted coconut flakes

MISO CARAMEL SAUCE
100 g (3½ oz) unsalted butter
125 ml (4 fl oz) single (pure/
   pouring) cream
175 g (6 oz) soft brown sugar
2 tsp pale (shiro) miso
1 tsp ground cinnamon

Scoop out four vanilla ice-cream balls and place in the freezer to set solid.

To make the miso caramel sauce, in a large frying pan heat the unsalted butter, cream and brown sugar. Cook over low heat until the sugar dissolves, then increase the heat to medium and simmer rapidly for 5 minutes or until thick. Add the miso and cinnamon and whisk through.

When close to serving, heat the caramel sauce and the waffles, peel the bananas and slice into coins.

Arrange the waffles on four plates. Top each with a ball of ice cream, then the bananas and caramel sauce. Sprinkle with the coconut and cashews.

NOTES

To toast the coconut, bake in an oven preheated to 170°C (325°F) or 150°C (300°F) fan forced for 8 minutes until golden at the edges.

You can use frozen waffles and heat them in the toaster or make a batch of your favourite recipe.

Pineapple upside-down cake has been around for almost a hundred years. Before decent cake tins were made for the home cook, people would have used iron frying pans. The fruit was cooked, covered with cake batter, baked and flipped over to serve. I've taken a riff on this classic by adding some Asian spices like star anise and cinnamon to the caramel. Serve it warm with a scoop of ice cream.

STAR ANISE PINEAPPLE UPSIDE-DOWN CAKE

SERVES 8
PREP 15 MINUTES
COOK 1 HOUR 5 MINUTES

300 g (10½ oz) unsalted
   butter, softened
160 g (5½ oz) soft brown sugar
4 tbsp golden or corn syrup
2 star anise
2 tsp ground cinnamon
1 tsp vanilla bean paste
1 small pineapple (450 g/1 lb flesh)
300 g (10½ oz) plain flour
2 tsp baking powder
200 g (7 oz) caster sugar
3 large eggs
1 tsp vanilla extract
100 ml (3½ fl oz) whole milk

crème fraîche, to serve

Preheat the oven to 180°C (350°F) or 160°C (315°F) fan forced.

Add 75 g (2½ oz) of the butter to a saucepan with the brown sugar and golden syrup. Heat until the sugar is melted, about 5 minutes. Remove from the heat. Grind the star anise in a spice mill, then stir into the butter with the cinnamon and vanilla paste.

Line the bottom of a 20 cm (8 inch) springform cake tin with baking paper so that the sugar syrup doesn't leak through the edges. Cut the pineapple into 1 cm (½ inch) thick slices and add to the tin.

In a mixing bowl, mix together the flour, baking powder and a pinch of salt.

In the bowl of a standing electric mixer or using a large bowl and an electric hand mixer, beat the caster sugar and remaining butter. Beat for 2–3 minutes and then add the eggs, one at a time, and the vanilla. Beat for 2 minutes until light and fluffy. Start to add the flour and alternate with milk until they are both incorporated. Beat for another minute until smooth.

Spoon the batter into the tin over the pineapple. Bake for 1 hour, covering with foil if it starts to brown. Let sit for 5 minutes and then turn out on a platter and serve warm as a pudding with crème fraîche. Alternatively, cool completely in the tin and serve as a cake.

Making your own chocolate bark is very simple and you can even melt the chocolate in the microwave. Try to use ordinary cooking chocolate as it melts more easily than very expensive brands with high cocoa percentages, which can split. Just be sure to keep the heat low and slow and you won't have any issues. The chilli bits work brilliantly with the salty nuts, chocolate and bursts of berries.

CHILLI CHOCOLATE NUT BARK WITH COCONUT

MAKES APPROX. 20 PIECES
**PREP 5 MINUTES, PLUS
10 MINUTES SETTING**
COOK 5 MINUTES

100 g (3½ oz) dark chocolate
100 g (3½ oz) milk chocolate
150 g (5½ oz) white chocolate
100 g (3½ oz) roasted
    salted cashews
1 tsp red chilli flakes
1 tsp sea salt
2 tbsp large toasted coconut
    flakes, chopped
3 tbsp freeze-dried strawberries
    or raspberries

Set two glass bowls over two saucepans of boiling water, making sure the water doesn't touch the bottom of the bowls.

Chop all the chocolates and melt the dark and milk in one bowl and the white in the other. Stir both until smooth. Alternatively, you can microwave either of them in short 30-second bursts and then stir with a rubber spatula. Usually the chocolate melts within 1 minute.

Line a baking tray with baking paper. Pour the chocolate onto the tray in patches and then marble together with a knife. Try to make it as thick as possible. Place the cashews, chilli, salt, coconut and berries over and let harden. It will harden much faster if placed in the refrigerator.

Break into pieces and serve.

NOTE

To toast the coconut, bake in an oven preheated to 170°C (325°F) or 150°C (300°F) fan forced for 8 minutes until golden at the edges.

Ice-cream sandwiches really need a soft biscuit to wrap around the filling to save your teeth! These chocolate biscuits are chewy and provide the perfect wrapper for this chilly, refreshing dessert. Try other flavours of ice cream like coconut, mango or pineapple.

CHOCOLATE MINT ICE-CREAM SANDWICHES

MAKES 10–12 SANDWICHES
PREP 30 MINUTES
COOK 10 MINUTES

125 g (4½ oz) butter,
   at room temperature
100 g (3½ oz) caster sugar
100 g (3½ oz) soft brown sugar
1 egg
1 tsp vanilla extract
125 g (4½ oz) plain flour
¼ tsp sea salt
45 g (1½ oz) cocoa powder
½ tsp bicarbonate of soda
   (baking soda)
75 g (2½ oz) chocolate chips

ICE-CREAM FILLING
500 ml (17 fl oz) mint chocolate chip
   ice cream

Preheat the oven to 180°C (350°F) or 160°C (315°F) fan forced.

In the bowl of a standing electric mixer or using an electric hand mixer and large bowl, beat the butter and two sugars until light and fluffy, about 2–3 minutes. Add the egg and vanilla and beat until incorporated. Add the flour, salt, cocoa powder and bicarbonate of soda and mix until smooth, about 1 minute. The dough will be slightly sticky, but that is because this recipe makes very flat, chewy cookies.

Line two baking trays with baking paper. Spoon 1 heaped tablespoon of the dough on each tray, pressing down so that they are slightly flatter. You should have 20–24 cookies. Bake the cookies for 6 minutes and then swap the trays around. Cook for another 6 minutes or until set but soft in the middle.

Remove from the oven and let cool on the trays for 5 minutes. The biscuits won't seem completely done and will be a little squishy, but they will finish cooking on the trays. Remove to a wire rack when set. They will keep in a covered container for 4 days.

Remove the ice cream from the freezer and let soften for a few minutes. Scoop one to two small balls of ice cream between two cookies and press to flatten. Place immediately in the freezer. When finished, cover the container of sandwiches and keep frozen until serving.

Not a trad Asian dessert, but this sharp lime cheesecake is perfect after lots of chillies, soy and ginger. A crisp base of biscuits and coconut is baked and the cream cheese is set with gelatine. The fruit you use on top is totally flexible, so choose what's in season.

LIME CHEESECAKE
WITH STRAWBERRIES

SERVES 8
PREP 30 MINUTES, PLUS 4 HOURS CHILLING
COOK 15 MINUTES

CRUST
150 g (5½ oz) crunchy biscuits, such as Hobnobs or ginger biscuits
30 g (1 oz) desiccated (grated dried) coconut
50 g (2 oz) butter, melted

FILLING
4 sheets gelatine (8 g/¼ oz)
1 tbsp boiling water
600 g (1 lb 5 oz) cream cheese
200 ml (7 fl oz) thick (double) cream
1 tsp vanilla bean paste
150 g (5½ oz) caster sugar
60 ml (2 fl oz) lime juice
1 tbsp lime zest

SAUCE AND TOPPINGS
100 g (3½ oz) caster sugar
100 ml (3½ fl oz) sweet dessert wine or prosecco (or water)
10 strawberries, hulled and halved
1 tbsp lime zest

Preheat the oven to 200°C (400°F) or 180°C (350°F) fan forced.

To make the crust, crush the biscuits in a food processor until a fine gravel texture. Mix in the coconut and butter. Press the mixture into an 18 cm (7 inch) springform tin (you can also use a 20 cm/8 inch one but it will be slightly flatter). Use a measuring cup or small water glass to help press it down and cover part of the sides. Bake for 8 minutes and then cool completely.

For the filling, place the gelatine sheets in a bowl of cold water and let sit until softened, about 5 minutes. Squeeze out the excess water and then cover with the boiling water. Let dissolve completely.

In the bowl of a standing electric mixer or using an electric hand mixer and a large bowl, beat the cream cheese until smooth. Pour in the cream, vanilla paste, sugar, liquid gelatine and lime juice and zest. Beat for 1 minute and then pour into the cooled crust. Cover with plastic wrap and chill for at least 4 hours or overnight.

For the sauce and toppings, in a small saucepan, pour in the sugar and wine and boil until syrupy, about 5 minutes. Let cool until lukewarm and then add the strawberries. Let it completely cool and when close to serving, pour over the cheesecake. Sprinkle with the lime zest.

NOTE

If you want to use powdered gelatine instead of the sheets, then substitute 1 tablespoon (1 sachet) mixed with 2 tablespoons water. Microwave for 30 seconds to melt and then pour into the mixture.

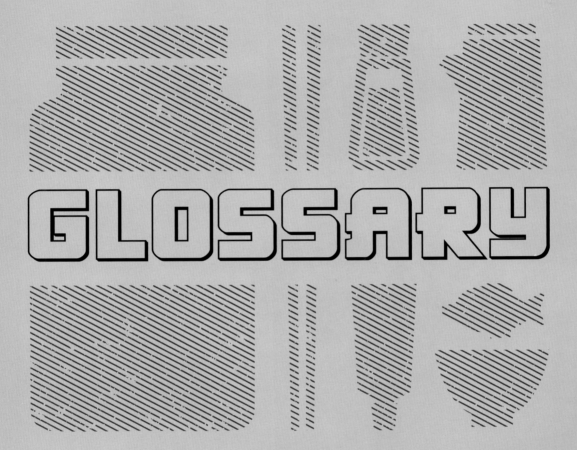

GLOSSARY

OILS

CHILLI OIL

Used across most Asian cuisines, this red-tinted oil is created by infusing dried chilli flakes and spices in vegetable oil. Ideal for stir-fries, peanut dressings and soups. La-yu is the Japanese version, but is a bit different as it's made with sesame oil.

COCONUT OIL

Cold-pressed from coconut flesh, this oil adds a delicate tropical flavour to cooking. It's sold in a solid form, but once heated it melts into a smooth liquid oil. Use it for curries or dehydrated vegetables like kale chips. Although its health benefits are exalted, it's still a pure saturated fat, so use it sparingly.

PEANUT AND VEGETABLE OIL

If you're deep or shallow frying, peanut (groundnut) is the best oil for its high smoking point and clean nutty taste. Generally it's more expensive so it's not for every day. When using other cooking oils, stay clear of bottles with generic names such as 'vegetable oil'. These are typically blended and are poor quality. Buy oils labelled as 'sunflower', 'rapeseed', 'corn oil' or a specific name as they will be pure and not mixed.

SESAME OIL

Prized for its nutty taste and high cooking temperature, sesame oil is ideal for stir-fries and dressings. The quality differs dramatically so look for 'pure sesame oil' instead of blended. If it's pale in colour, chances are it's not 100 percent sesame, so choose the darker coloured ones. It's best to buy small bottles as the aroma dissipates quickly. If you have room in your refrigerator, store it there.

SUGARS

PALM SUGAR

Used in South East Asian cooking, palm sugar has a fudgey, caramel taste that is far superior to other processed sugars. It's made from the boiled sap of Palmyra palm tree flowers and then cooked until thick. Avoid the dry, hard discs that are difficult to chop and buy the soft variety in plastic tubs. It's indispensable for Thai and Vietnamese dressings, glazes and hot pots. Once opened, refrigerate to avoid mould.

ROCK SUGAR

These Chinese yellow-hued chunks of sugar are made by crystallising sugar. When boiled down, rock sugar adds a sticky texture and red colour to meats like char sui pork. You can substitute regular caster sugar, but it's not quite the same. Before heating, crush the sugar up in a mortar and pestle so it melts faster.

COCONUT

COCONUT MILK/CREAM

Produced by blending the white coconut flesh with water and straining out the liquid. When left to settle, the coconut cream rises to the top. You can buy separate tins of the cream or the milk – just shake it up and it's ready to use. Recipes will call specifically for one or the other.

DESICCATED COCONUT

Coconut flesh that's finely shredded and dried is called desiccated. It's also sold in bigger pieces, which are known as coconut flakes. Sprinkled into curries, salads and sweets, it imparts an exotic taste. Be sure not to buy sweetened coconut, which is purely used for baking.

CHILLI

CURRY PASTES

Enter any Asian food store and you will see an aisle of curry pastes sold in plastic tubs. The quality is very high and they are really useful to have in your refrigerator. Most share a base of lemongrass, galangal, ginger, garlic, makrut (kaffir lime) leaves, shrimp paste, shallots, garlic and ground spices like cumin and coriander. Thai red curry paste has the addition of both reconstituted dried and fresh bird's eye chillies. A variation of this is Malaysian Penang red curry paste, which is slightly less hot, sweeter and sometimes has ground peanuts. Massaman Thai curry paste has Islamic influences with the addition of Middle Eastern spices like cloves and cinnamon. It's used to make the rich curry with the same name that includes potatoes, meat and peanuts. Yellow curry paste is a Thai paste that's more sour than the red variety and has Indian curry powder and turmeric added. It's sometimes called sour curry paste. Green curry paste is a famous Thai recipe that uses copious green chillies, lime leaves and coriander (cilantro) to give it a bright green colour.

NAM PRIK

Also called Thai chilli jam or paste, this roasted chilli sauce is made from chillies, shallots, garlic, tamarind and shrimp paste. It's the quintessential taste of tom yum soup and is extremely useful for quick Thai stir-fry sauces. Keep refrigerated once opened and dollop it into soups, curries or peanut sauces.

ROASTED CHILLI FLAKES IN OIL

Chiu chow chilli oil or crispy chilli oil are both names used for chilli oil. You can use the red oil floating on top for cooking, but the real treasure lies below in the tasty bits or 'gunk'. Lao Gan Ma is a legendary Chinese brand with the additions of shallots, Sichuan peppercorns and black beans. The iconic red bottle with the old Chinese lady on its label has a cult following globally. It's indispensable in Asian cooking as a dipping sauce for dumplings, added to stir-fries or dolloped into noodle soups or curries. I simply couldn't live without it and neither should you.

RED CHILLI SAUCE

Most commonly, red chilli sauce is used as a dipping sauce for fried food. Technically sriracha is a red chilli sauce, but it is spicier than its Chinese and Malaysian cousins. The latter tend to be much sweeter, have more ingredients like ginger and aren't hot at all.

SAMBAL OELEK

The simplest of the Indonesian/Malaysian sambal chilli sauces, this is blended from red chillies, vinegar and salt. It's perfect for when you want to mix up a quick dipping sauce or marinade without chopping up fresh chillies. There are many more complicated sambals that involve the additions of lemongrass, garlic, makrut (kaffir lime) leaves, tamarind, dried shrimp paste, onions or ginger, but this one is a refrigerator staple.

SRIRACHA

A spicy Thai red chilli sauce made from finely blended chillies, sugar, garlic and vinegar. Used as a dipping sauce, for making spicy mayonnaise, blended into stir-fry sauces or spooned over bowls of noodle soup, it's a firm fixture in many people's refrigerators around the world. It's extremely spicy, so if you're using it as a dipping sauce, mix it with some rice vinegar to temper its heat.

SOY

The cornerstone of all Asian cooking, soy sauce is produced from fermented soya beans, rice and mould. Each country has its own distinct flavour that suits its cuisine. Shoyu (Japanese) soy sauce is sweeter and cleaner, while Chinese and Thai soy sauces tend to be on the saltier side. Tamari is a wheat-free soy sauce, but has a stronger flavour so use in smaller amounts. In a perfect world you might stock all of them depending on what you are cooking, but see what your cupboards can hold.

LIGHT SOY SAUCE

Both the Chinese and Thai refer to regular soy sauce as light or thin soy. It tastes saltier than Japanese varieties, which brand 'light' as a reduced-salt version. Use light soy sauce for all types of cooking, such as dressings, marinades, stir-fry sauces and braises.

DARK SOY SAUCE

Used mainly for cooking or marinades, dark soy is less salty, but needs heat to bring out the flavour. It's made the same way as light soy, but is mixed with molasses and aged for longer. It shouldn't be used for dipping sauces or recipes where it isn't heated.

SWEET SOY SAUCE (KECAP MANIS)

Made from fermented black soya beans, grain, mould and palm sugar, this has a much thicker consistency and sweeter taste than regular soy. The Thais refer to it as 'sweet soy sauce' and Malaysia/Indonesia brand it under 'kecap manis'. You can use both products interchangeably. It's an extremely valued condiment for instant dipping sauces, dressings, stir-fry sauce or marinades balanced out with a little rice vinegar, chilli or lime.

THAI BLACK SOY SAUCE

There are two Thai cooking sauces that can be easily confused. Thai sweet soy sauce (see ew waan) is similar to kecap manis and can be utilised in the same way. Thai black soy sauce (see ew dam) is more intense in its salt and sugar taste and is used for specific Thai sauces and stir-fries.

HOISIN SAUCE

An indispensable Chinese condiment that is used for dipping sauce, glazes, BBQ sauce and stir-fries. Made from yellow soya beans, chilli, five-spice powder, garlic and vinegar, its rich sweet-and-salty taste suits a wide variety of Asian dishes.

THAI SEASONING SAUCE

One of Thailand's secret sauces, this is made from fermented soya beans, salt and sugar. Although it doesn't list MSG as an ingredient, it has 'flavour enhancer', which might explain the umami boost when used in stir-fries. Think of it like Worcestershire sauce – it makes everything taste good. It can be used as a vegetarian or vegan alternative to fish sauce.

FERMENTED

GOCHUJANG (KOREAN CHILLI PASTE)

A sticky Korean chilli paste sold in plastic tubs, gochujang has a thick, glossy consistency. Its ingredients include red chilli powder, rice powder, sugar and fermented soya beans. Mixed with rice vinegar and sugar, it's the mouthwatering sauce for bibimbap and Korean fried chicken. The complex sweet-and-spicy flavours complement stir-fries, noodles, stews and soups, but it's also dazzling mixed into mayonnaise for burgers and tacos or drizzled over fried food.

MISO

There are many varieties of miso paste, but there are only two that you will mainly use. The pale yellow shiro miso is perfect for dressings and soups and has a mild, sweet, salty taste. Aka (red) is the more assertive of the two because it's fermented for longer. It's best used in small amounts for glazes or BBQ sauce. Koreans use a miso paste called doenjang, which is a coarse soya bean paste. It's mixed with gochujang chilli paste to make the famous ssamjang sauce that is served with grilled bulgogi and lettuce wraps. Once opened, miso should be refrigerated.

SALTED BLACK BEANS

Not to be confused with black bean sauce, these are dried, fermented black soya beans that are used to make the sauce. Sold as shrivelled, whole salted beans, they are used in the famous mapo dofu and stir-fry sauces and are added to glazes for steamed pork ribs and other meats. The quality is far superior to jars of gloopy black bean sauce, but use them sparingly as their intense funky taste goes far.

SWEET BEAN SAUCE

Sometimes called sweet wheat paste, this fermented wheat, sugar and salt paste is sweeter than yellow soya bean paste, but is used in the same types of Chinese dishes. There is also an entirely different product called sweet bean paste made with adzuki beans, which is used to make sweet dessert buns.

THAI FERMENTED SOYA BEAN SAUCE (TAO JIEW)

Sold in tall bottles near the fish sauce, this is the Thai equivalent of miso or Chinese yellow soya bean paste, but is more liquid. Use it in stir-fries, chilli sauces for soups or dipping sauces.

TOBAN JIANG (HOT CHILLI BEAN PASTE)

Also called toban djan or doubanjiang, this chilli bean sauce is produced from fermented broad beans, salt, rice, chillies and spices. Fiery hot and deliciously salty, its the key ingredient for mapo dofu, soup, noodles, stir-fries and braises. Used prevalently in Chinese cooking, it's also loved by the Japanese who mix it into ramen, miso glazes and hot pots. Once opened, keep refrigerated.

YELLOW SOYA BEAN PASTE

Made from soya beans, wheat and salt, this brownish paste is used in the famous Zhajiang mian – minced (ground) pork noodles. Its salty depth is also good mixed into dipping sauces or in red braised meats or poultry. You could substitute pale miso paste (shiro) if you can't find it.

UMEBOSHI (PICKLED PLUMS)

These potent Japanese sour pickled plums resemble wizened apricots and are eaten as a snack or as part of onigiri (rice balls with nori) for breakfast or lunch. After picking, they are packed in salt and weighted down to press out the liquid. They possess a very high level of citric acid and are purported to have many health benefits, such as warding off colds, stopping ageing and curing hangovers. You can use the mashed paste to make delicious dressings, sauces and glazes for meat. Buy umeboshi plums as a paste in jars or the whole plums. The latter cost a bit more, but are better quality and have a sweeter taste.

##

BONITO FLAKES

Sometimes labelled katsuobushi, bonito flakes is another name for the skipjack tuna they are produced from. The fish is dried, smoked and fermented with koji mould until rock hard. The process can take anywhere from 2 months up to 2 years. The blocks of petrified fish are then shaved into feathery paper-thin slices to use in dashi or sprinkle over agadashi tofu or okonomiyaki. Along with kombu seaweed, they are what make dashi stock so flavourful. Keep unopened bags in your cupboard for up to a year.

DRIED SHRIMP

Blitzed into Chinese XO sauce, pounded into Thai green papaya salad, boiled into a Korean soup or whizzed into Malay curry pastes, dried shrimp feature prominently in Asian cooking. Tiny sweet fresh prawns (shrimp) are sun-dried until shrunken and then packaged in an airtight bag. Once opened, place in a tight-fitting lidded jar to contain lingering odours in your refrigerator.

FISH SAUCE

Used in every Asian country (even Japan), fish sauce is a 'top five' store-cupboard ingredient that's hard to replicate. Made from fermented anchovies and salt, it adds a salty depth of flavour and magic taste to food. Mixed with lime, chillies and sugar, it transforms to nuac cham, the ubiquitous dipping sauce of South East Asia, but its talents go much further than that in all aspects of Asian cooking.

OYSTER SAUCE

Oyster juices are simmered and caramelised with the addition of sugar, soy and cornflour to produce this glorious sauce. Stir-fry sauces take on an extra depth of flavour from its salty-fishy aroma and it's perfect in glazes and BBQ sauces. Look for a good brand like Thai Maekrua, which is brewed with fresh oyster juices, versus other artificially manufactured bottles.

SHRIMP PASTE

Kapi (Thai) or belacan (Malaysian) are the most common names you will see for this potent, pungent and salty ingredient. Small prawns (shrimp) are ground with salt, sun-dried and packed into small plastic containers. You might wonder how such a foul-smelling ingredient can add such a tremendous depth of flavour, but it's all down to the magic of the umami/salty/fishy elements. Kapi is used in blended curry pastes and chilli jams and pounded into sauces for Indonesian and Malaysian dishes. Shrimp paste is very intense, so err on the side of small amounts.

SOUR

BLACK VINEGAR
The Chinese name for this dark, smoky tasting vinegar is Chinkiang. A very important ingredient in Asian cooking, it's hard to replicate its unique character. Made from black glutinous rice, it adds a tangy, sweet malt flavour to dressings, noodle dishes, dipping sauces for dumplings and braises.

MIRIN
Made from rice wine and similar to sake, although mirin has less alcohol and more sugar. It's the ideal ingredient for thinning out and balancing other salty ingredients like soy or miso. Used in all aspects of Japanese cooking, it's a must-have for your cupboard.

RICE VINEGAR
Japanese rice vinegar, also called rice wine vinegar, is a pale yellow colour and has a mild, sweet flavour compared to western vinegars. Chinese rice vinegar is a white clear colour, very acidic and is not the preferred product to use. Use the Japanese for dressings, dipping sauces, braises and all types of cooking.

SAKE
This rice wine is produced by fermenting polished rice and is brewed predominately in the Hyogo prefecture on Honshu island. The water contains special minerals that aid in the production. Not only an alcohol to be sipped hot or cold, sake is used in a wide range of Japanese cooking. Similar to mirin, it brings a balance to sauces.

SHAOXING RICE WINE
Sometimes spelled Shaohsing, Chinese rice wine is used for braises like the famous red-cooked pork belly or in stir-fry sauces and marinades. Produced by fermenting glutinous rice, it tastes more like sherry than sake. It's an essential ingredient for Chinese cooking and should be easy to find in most supermarkets.

TAMARIND
Tamarind adds a sour depth to curries, glazes, dipping sauces and stir-fries. It's paramount that you have this in your refrigerator to use this book. I can't stress that enough. It makes everything taste balanced and connects the dots between sweet and sour, salty and spicy. The paste is made from the sticky pulp of pods of large tropical trees. Either it's packed with all of the seeds in bars or in jars already sieved and ready to go. It's sold under the names tamarind purée or tamarind paste. If it looks particularly thick, then thin it back with some water. Every brand is slightly different.

YUZU
This spectacular tangerine-sized citrus fruit grows in Japan, Korea and China. It's prized for its floral and aromatic juice, which tastes like a cross between lime and grapefruit. Pour it over sashimi or mix it into dressings and dipping sauces. The juice is sold in bottles that need to be refrigerated. If you can't find it, you can use equal parts grapefruit and lime juice. The peel is either candied, dried for spice mixes or pounded with green or red chillies and salt to make the delicious yuzu kosho paste. This fiery condiment is used to grill meat and fish and spoon into ramen or hot pots.

JAPANESE

DRIED SHIITAKE MUSHROOMS
Predominantly used in Japanese, Chinese and Korean cooking, these dehydrated umami-rich mushrooms have a rich depth. Add them to vegan stock, dashi or chicken broth along with kombu for a smoky flavour. Use the softened mushrooms to make pickles or add to stir-fries, spring rolls and soups.

HOT YELLOW MUSTARD (KARASHI)
Sold in plastic tubes similar to wasabi, this Japanese mustard is a fiery condiment that's most well known for being served with tonkatsu (panko fried pork). I like squirting a tiny amount of it into miso dressings or dipping sauces for a spicy kick. You can substitute English hot mustard if you can't find it.

KEWPIE MAYONNAISE
With a global cult following, this creamy yellow Japanese mayonnaise is packaged in a squeezy bottle with a star-shaped nozzle. Made with plenty of egg yolks and rice vinegar, it adds a real tanginess to dipping sauces or can be made into a dressing for potato salads. Traditionally, the mayonnaise is used for drizzling over takoyaki (crispy octopus balls) and okonomiyaki pancakes.

KOMBU SEAWEED
A key component for making dashi stock, kombu is a black-hued dehydrated kelp that's harvested off the coast of Japan. It's sold in flat, broad pieces that will keep in your cupboard for a long time. Once softened, it turns a dark green colour and can be chopped up for miso soup or salad with rice vinegar.

NORI
The shiny, green/black paper used to wrap sushi is made from seaweed shredded to a paste and then pressed into sheets. It's sold in different grades with the lightest green colour being the poorest quality up to the darkest green/black being the best. Use leftover sheets to roast over an open flame, crumble and sprinkle over noodles, salads, rice and okonomiyaki.

WASABI
The sharp, nostril-flaring accompaniment to sushi, wasabi paste is produced from grinding the root of the wasabi japonica plant. But that's not the product most of us are spreading on our sushi. Typically it's a commercial paste made from ground horseradish, mustard and green colouring. The true pure wasabi is rarer and far softer in taste.

SPICE MIXES

BLACK AND WHITE SESAME SEEDS

Essential for all types of Asian cooking, sesame seeds add a nutty taste, texture and a beautiful garnish to foods. They're grown on a sesame plant and the only difference is the white have the outer husk removed. The black ones are pre-roasted before packing, so no need to toast before using. To toast the white seeds, place in a dry non-stick frying pan and leave the flame on the lowest possible setting. Let them slowly turn golden, shaking often, for 10 minutes. I usually make a big batch and then keep them refrigerated in a lidded jar. If using in dressings or soups, grind while warm in a mortar and pestle.

CURRY POWDER

This Indian spice mix can contain anything from five to thirty different ground spices. The Japanese brand S & B is very good and the Vietnamese make their own special recipe, which contains annatto powder. Curry powder is used widely across all Asian cooking. For the sake of simplicity, I would suggest buying a very mild yellow-coloured curry powder, such as Madras. Avoid using heavy spiced varieties like garam masala.

DRIED RED CHILLIES

There is an enormous variety of dried red chillies so you don't need to concentrate on the names so much as the size and depth of colour. The smaller the chilli, the hotter it will be and the inverse is true for the big ones. Their skins should be shiny and flexible so stay clear of brown, brittle dried chillies, which are old and bitter. When making curries, it's easier to work with bigger chillies for deseeding and soaking. I sometimes use Mexican chillies for their large size, intense flavour and freshness. For stir-fries where the chillies are included whole, try to order small Sichuan chillies. You can get them through Amazon or Asian online stores and they have a unique fragrance that suits their cuisine. Store your dried chillies in a zip lock bag refrigerated. This will preserve the oil in the skins as long as possible.

FIVE-SPICE POWDER

A classic ingredient for making Peking duck or pork belly, five-spice is particularly loved by the Chinese and Taiwanese. BBQ sauces, glazes, marinades and braises all rely on its exotic combination. Although there are many variations of this powder, there are generally five spices used: star anise, cloves, cinnamon, Sichuan peppercorns and fennel seeds.

FURIKAKI

This umami-loaded Japanese dry seasoning comes in countless variations. Typically it contains crushed bonito fish flakes or some fishy component, nori, sesame seeds, chilli, dried egg and yeast extract. On paper that doesn't sound flavourful, but it's truly delicious sprinkled on rice, salads, eggs and over soup. It's also a wonderful seasoning for tofu before rolling in cornflour and shallow frying.

GOCHUGARU (KOREAN CHILLI FLAKES)

Korean chilli flakes are essential for making kimchee, bulgogi and other marinades. Made from chillies dried in the sun, they are seeded first and then roughly ground. With the seeds removed, they are not overly spicy and have a smoky, fruity taste. Use them for any dish that requires dried chillies. It's easiest to buy them online from an Asian store or Amazon.

SICHUAN PEPPERCORNS

There isn't a substitute for this unique tongue-tingling berry grown in China. It's used heavily in Sichuan and the northern provinces' cooking, providing a numbing citrus taste sensation. Mapo dofu, Xian lamb skewers, salt and pepper prawns and dan dan noodles are just some of the dishes that celebrate this famous spice. To achieve the best flavour, heat the peppercorns in a dry frying pan for about 30 seconds until fragrant, and then roughly grind in a mortar and pestle.

STAR ANISE

A star-shaped spice, which is the dried fruit of a Chinese tree. Coveted for its wonderful liquorice and sweet anise aroma, star anise is used in braises, soups and sauces in most parts of Asia. It's one of the main spices found in five-spice powder.

TOGARASHI (SHICHIMI TOGARASHI)

Its name translates to 'seven-flavour chilli' and refers to the number of ingredients used to make this seasoning mix. Typically it contains chilli, orange peel, black and white sesame seeds, sansho pepper, ginger, seaweed and hemp seed, but different brands will vary. It's indispensable as a condiment for Japanese ramen, noodles, salads and rice. Sprinkle it over roast chicken wings, pork chops and grilled steak and experience its magic taste. If you can't find it, substitute an equal mix of mild ground chilli powder, lemon zest and toasted sesame seeds.

WHITE PEPPERCORNS

Grown from the same pepper plant as black peppercorns, white have the outer husk removed. As a result they are less overwhelming, but maintain a clean, sharp heat. They are used in all types of Asian cooking and hot-and-sour soup wouldn't be the same without this essential spice.

FLOURS

CORNFLOUR

Cornflour, or cornstarch, is a fine flour that is dissolved in water to thicken stir-fry sauces and braises. It's particularly good for coating meat, tofu or fish before deep frying. Compared to plain (all-purpose) flour, it imparts a much crispier crust.

POTATO FLOUR

Potato flour is sometimes labelled 'potato starch' or 'katakuriko' (Japanese). It's used exactly like cornflour: to thicken sauces or for flour dredging before deep-frying. Recipes like karaage (Japanese fried chicken) or Taiwanese popcorn chicken get their ultra-crisp coating from this velvet flour, but you can use cornflour as well. I've tried both and potato flour comes out a little better.

RICE FLOUR

Made from ground long-grain rice, this is used in the same way as the two flours above. Be sure not to buy 'glutinous rice flour', which is an entirely different product that's used for sweets and some dumpling wrappers. I like to mix rice flour with potato or cornflour for an uber-fried food coating. It's particularly good for fried squid or prawns. Thai cooking uses rice flour to sprinkle over larbs or other salads, but that's done with whole rice that's toasted and roughly ground.

FRESH

CHILLIES

Fresh chillies are rated for their fieriness on the Scoville heat scale. It's still debatable what the hottest chilli in the world is, but the Carolina reaper is said to be right near the top with a rating of 1.5 million Scoville units. It's vital to use the right type and size of chilli or it can destroy your cooking efforts. Most of my recipes use thumb-sized red chillies and those are usually Fresno or serenade chillies. The green are either serenade or jalapeño with the latter being darker and rounder. Both have a heat of about 2500 to 8000 on the scale, so are perfect for cooking. Thai bird's eye chillies (aka 'scuds') are very powerful with a rating of 100 000 to 225 000 on the scale, but can be used in small amounts as they are authentic to Thai cooking. If you scrape out the seeds and membranes, it removes the majority of heat, but if you're using a scorcher like a Scotch bonnet or habanero, it's still going to blow everyone's head off.

CHINESE CELERY

Although you can substitute the normal variety, Chinese celery has much finer stems and an intense celery taste. It's used in salads, tofu dishes and noodle hot pots. Both the leaves and stems can be used.

CORIANDER AND OTHER HERBS

Unlike other herbs where the stems and roots are discarded, coriander (cilantro) is prized for every part. The most intense section are the roots, which are ground into curries or pounded with garlic and black peppercorns to marinate meats or form the base for stir-fries. The stems and leaves are used for salads, fresh spring rolls and garnishing finished dishes. In South East Asia, herbs like coriander, sweet basil, mint and dill (mostly Vietnam) are heavily featured and used like salad leaves in western cooking.

GALANGAL/GINGER/TURMERIC

These three root-based plants are from the rhizome family. Galangal has a pronounced pine, medicinal citrus aroma with a tough skin that needs to removed with a knife. Predominately it is blended in curry pastes, but is also used to flavour soups like tom yum. Ginger is used in all Asian cooking and, like garlic, is a cornerstone ingredient. Fresh turmeric is blitzed into curry pastes, particularly the sour yellow.

LEMONGRASS

Part of the grass family, lemongrass is a tropical herb with an intense lemon taste. South East Asian cooking relies on it as a key ingredient for curry pastes, soups, salads and marinades. The outer husk needs to be removed so first chop the ends off and use the lower third of the stem. Use something heavy like a stone mortar or tin to pound it once or twice and then peel away the tough layers. Finely chop the remaining tender heart or it won't finely grind in a food processor or blender.

MAKRUT LIME ZEST AND LEAVES

This Asian citrus, also known as kaffir lime, is prized for its skin and the leaves that grow alongside. It has an intense lime flavour and both the leaves and zest are used in curry pastes, fish cakes and salads. If using leaves in a curry, add near the end of cooking to retain the citrus essence. Keep frozen in an airtight container.

SPRING ONIONS

These members of the allium family go by many different names: scallions, spring onions, salad onions or green onions. The Japanese call them 'negi' and the Asian variety are thinner and much longer. They are used in most Asian cuisines in fried rice, stir-fries, salads and, most importantly, as a garnish.

THAI BASIL

Thai sweet basil has a sweet anise/liquorice aroma and is used as a garnish in soups, larbs, salads and curries in Thai and Vietnamese cooking. Most supermarkets carry it or you can source it online. Holy basil is used for cooked dishes, like pad krapow gai stir-fry. It's more difficult to find so I usually end up using Thai basil instead.

THAI SHALLOTS

Also named Asian shallots or Thai red onions, these tiny purple-skinned alliums have a sharper taste than western shallots. Their lower water content also makes them ideal for frying crisp. When used raw in salads and dipping sauces, their sweet flavour and deep colour is appealing. Buy at Asian shops or online or you can substitute small French shallots.

iNDEX